Nothing to Lose

NOTHING TO LOSE

a play by David Fennario

Vancouver, Talonbooks, 1977

copyright © 1977 David Fennario

published with assistance from the Canada Council

Talonbooks
201 1019 East Cordova
Vancouver
British Columbia V6A 1M8
Canada

This book was typeset by Linda Gilbert of B.C. Monthly Typesetting Service, designed by David Robinson and printed by Hemlock Printers for Talonbooks.

First printing: December 1977

Talonplays are edited by Peter Hay.

Canadian Cataloguing in Publication Data

  Fennario, David, 1947—
  Nothing to lose

  ISBN 0-88922-121-9

  1. Title.
  PS8561.E54N6   C812'.5'4   C77-002252-9
  PR9199.3.F45N6

Nothing to Lose was commissioned by and first performed at Centaur Theatre in Montreal, Quebec, on November 11, 1976, with the following cast:

Claude	Denys Nadon
Chabougamou	Jean Archambault
Foreman	Tony Angelo
Gros Gas	Raymond Belisle
Fred	Walter Bolton
Murray	Lubomyr Mykytiuk
Jerry	Don Scanlan
Jackie	Peter MacNeill
Frank	Simon Malbogat

Directed by Guy Sprung
Designed by Barbara Matis
Lighting by Harry Frehner

Nothing to Lose was also performed by Toronto Workshop Productions at Toronto Free Theatre in Toronto, Ontario as a Centaur Theatre Production on January 17, 1978, with the following cast:

Claude	Denys Nadon
Chabougamou	Jean Archambault
Foreman	Tony Angelo
Gros Gas	Andre Saint-Denis
Fred	Ray Landry
Murray	Lubomyr Mykytiuk
Jerry	Don Scanlan
Jackie	Peter MacNeill
Frank	Simon Malbogat

Directed by Guy Sprung
Designed by Barbara Matis
Lighting by Harry Frehner

The scene is a wintertime tavern in the Point
Saint Charles working class district of Montreal
across the street from Sunnybrook Farm's
warehouse.

CLAUDE, the waiter, enters from one side of
the tavern pushing CHABOUGAMOU, the bar
drunk, in front of him.

CLAUDE:
  Là-bas! Hey, là-bas, tabarnac!

CHABOUGAMOU: *stopping at one of the tables*
  Ici, Claude? Ici?

CLAUDE:
  Non, pas ici, further back than that. Là-bas!

CHABOUGAMOU: *moving to a back table*
  Okay, Claude? Deux bières. Deux bières, Claude.

He hands CLAUDE a handful of pennies.

CLAUDE: *counting the pennies*
Tabarnac, c'est trente sous.

CHABOUGAMOU:
C'est okay, Claude?

CLAUDE:
Non, c'est pas okay. Trente-cinq sous, câlice!

CHABOUGAMOU: *digging into his pocket and handing
CLAUDE a nickel* Deux, Claude. Deux.

CLAUDE puts two beers down on his table.

CLAUDE:
Don't drink too fast, eh?

CHABOUGAMOU:
Okay, Claude. Okay.

The FOREMAN enters and sits down.

CLAUDE:
Pas de bruit.

FOREMAN:
Gimme a beer, Claude.

CLAUDE:
Yes, sir.

*He gets a beer and goes and puts it down on the
FOREMAN's table.*

Trente-cinq.

The FOREMAN pays him.

FOREMAN:
Good game last night, eh?

CLAUDE: *taking a tip*
Merci. Ah oui, good game. Christ, you saw it?

FOREMAN:
Yeah, Canadiens won again.

CLAUDE:
Hey, twelve games in a row. Lafleur, he's good, eh?

FOREMAN:
Yeah.

CLAUDE:
Just like the Rocket.

CHABOUGAMOU:
Oui, Claude, oui. Good game, good game, the Expos.

CLAUDE:
The Expos?

CHABOUGAMOU:
They shoot, they score, eh?

CLAUDE:
Hey, Ti-Cul.

CHABOUGAMOU:
First base, right down the ice. Good score.

CLAUDE: *walking away*
Dat guy, deux choses dans la même roule, eh?

CHABOUGAMOU:
Okay, Claude, okay. C'est vrai. Me, I know.

> *CLAUDE goes over and arranges the latest*
> *Mini-Loto number on the Mini-Loto board.*
> *The sound of trucks is heard and a police car*
> *passing by with the siren wailing.*

CLAUDE: *looking at his Mini-Loto ticket*
Tabarnac!

FOREMAN:
Win some, lose some, eh?

CLAUDE:
Oui, that's for sure.

CHABOUGAMOU:
That's for sure.

> *JERRY enters carrying a plastic book satchel
> and wearing sunglasses. He takes off his sunglasses
> and passes through to the other side of the
> tavern. He returns and sits down one table away
> from the FOREMAN.*

CLAUDE: *going over to JERRY*
Oui, qu'est-que tu veux?

JERRY:
Hi, Claude.

CLAUDE:
I know you?

JERRY:
Yeah. I used to sit over there with old Joe Côté,
remember?

CLAUDE:
Uh, maybe. You want two beers?

JERRY:
Uh, yeah. Hey, how is the old guy?

CLAUDE:
Old Joe Côté? He don't come here for a long time.
I think his legs are bad. Two beers?

JERRY:
Yeah. Hey, what about Jackie Robinson? Works across the street there at Sunnybrook's.

CLAUDE:
Which Jack? Big Jack or Crazy Jack?

JERRY:
Uh, Crazy Jack.

CLAUDE:
Oh, yeah, he comes here. You his friend?

JERRY:
Yeah.

CLAUDE:
That guy, he's crazy.

He exits to the other side of the tavern.

CHABOUGAMOU looks around, sees JERRY and goes over and sits down at his table. He puts his fingers to his mouth to indicate that he wants a cigarette.

CHABOUGAMOU:
Cigarette? Hey, cigarette?

JERRY:
Yeah, sure.

He passes CHABOUGAMOU a cigarette.

There ya go. Wanna light? Un feu?

CHABOUGAMOU:
   Sure.

   He puts the cigarette in his mouth.

   You smart guy, eh, toi?

JERRY:
   Hey, turn it around. Hey, the filter. You're smoking the wrong end. The filter.

CHABOUGAMOU:
   Huh? Don't worry about dat.

   He breaks off the filter and flips it over his shoulder. It lands on the FOREMAN's table. JERRY lights his cigarette.

   You want something, eh? Eh, toi? Smart guy. I know what you tink.

JERRY:
   Ya do, eh?

CHABOUGAMOU:
   This is the place, eh? This is not the place. Pas la place.

JERRY:
   Oh, yeah?

CHABOUGAMOU:
   Me, I'm not from Chabougamou. Me, I'm from Rivière du Loup.

JERRY:
   Rivière du Loup, eh?

CHABOUGAMOU:
I know what you tink, smart guy.

CLAUDE enters with JERRY's beer.

Hey, Claude, deux.

CLAUDE:
Non.

He puts the beer down on JERRY'S table.

Soixante-dix.

CHABOUGAMOU: *holding up two fingers*
Deux, Claude. I pay you tomorrow, okay?

CLAUDE:
Ferme ta gueule, toi.

JERRY pays him for the beer.

Merci.

*CLAUDE moves over to the bar where he sits
down on a stool and reads a newspaper.*

CHABOUGAMOU:
Pas Chabougamou, moi. Rivière du Loup. Remember
that.

FOREMAN:
Hey, why don't you go back?

CHABOUGAMOU:
Hey, I know you too, eh?

JERRY exits to the washroom.

While he is not there, CHABOUGAMOU grabs
one of his beers, pours half of it into his glass
and goes back to his table.

MURRAY enters, looks around and sits down.

JERRY: *re-entering, back at his table, looking at his half-*
empty glass of beer What's this? Evaporation or what?

CLAUDE: *coming over to serve MURRAY*
Long time, no see, Murray.

MURRAY:
Yeah, how's things, Claude?

CLAUDE:
Comme ci, comme ça. You want two beers?

MURRAY:
No, I'm back on my diet.

CLAUDE:
A what?

MURRAY:
A diet, but I guess you don't know about that, eh?
Ha, ha, only kidding, Claude. Listen, give me some
orange juice.

CLAUDE:
Orange juice?

MURRAY:
Okay, forget it. I'm just here to meet Gros Gas and
Fred.

CHABOUGAMOU: *singing*
You musta been a beautiful baby,
'Cause, baby, look at you now. . . .

You know that one, huh? Huh?

CLAUDE: *exiting*
Hey, hey, Chabougamou, ferme ta gueule.

CHABOUGAMOU:
Pas Chabougamou, moi. Rivière du Loup, hostie.

*MURRAY looks at his watch, then goes over to
the telephone and dials a number.*

MURRAY:
Yes, hi, sweetheart. Give me extension 361. Yeah,
hello, John Shaeffer please. Hello, John? Murray
Friedman here. Yeah, that's right. Yeah, I know
there's an important meeting this afternoon, but
look, I'm gonna be late. Can't help it, John. Listen,
got a call from Warehouse 28 this morning. Yeah,
more shit kicking, right. Might be trouble. They got
a new foreman here they don't like and they're
threatening another walkout. Ahuh. Well, what
can I say? They're pissed off. Yeah, yeah, I'm gonna
talk to Pacquette and that other guy. What's his
name? Roman. Yeah, George Roman. Don't worry,
I know these guys. I know them. I used to work here.
Listen, don't worry, they won't break the contract.
Ahuh. Okay, don't worry. You want the number
here? It's uh, 931-7768. Office number is 931-0806.
Right. Soon as possible.

*He hangs up the telephone and writes in his
notebook.*

Roman. George Roman.

FOREMAN:
Hey. Hey, you.

MURRAY:
Huh? Who, me?

FOREMAN:
Yeah, come here. Come here.

15

MURRAY: *going over to him*
    Yeah?

FOREMAN:
    You're the union guy, eh?

MURRAY:
    Uh, yeah.

FOREMAN:
    That's nice.

MURRAY:
    Huh?

FOREMAN:
    That's nice.

MURRAY:
    Yeah, okay.

FOREMAN:
    You do your job, I do mine. No problems.

MURRAY:
    Right, no problems.

    He shrugs and goes back to his table.

    Schmuck!

    CLAUDE enters and goes over to MURRAY with a can of tomato juice.

CLAUDE:
    Trente-cinq.

MURRAY:
    What's that?

CLAUDE:
Juice. You asked for juice.

MURRAY:
Orange juice. I asked for orange juice.

CLAUDE:
That's right, juice.

MURRAY:
I don't want it.

CLAUDE:
Hey, it's too late now. I opened it.

MURRAY:
Hey, Claude.

CLAUDE:
Hey, that's the law, Murray. You know that.

MURRAY:
Alright, alright.

CLAUDE:
It's not me, it's the boss.

MURRAY:
Yeah, yeah. Trente-cinq?

CLAUDE:
Trente-cinq.

MURRAY:
You want a tip too?

He pays him.

CLAUDE:
Sure, merci.

He goes back to his newspaper.

MURRAY: *picking up the can of tomato juice and reading the label* What's in this? Salt. Just salt?

> *GROS GAS and FRED enter carrying their lunch bags.*

FRED:
We walk out, they'll fire us for sure.

GROS GAS:
No, no, no.

FRED:
That's what I heard.

GROS GAS:
That's what you hear, but that's not what they do. Hey, that's bullshit from the ass, Fred.

FRED:
I dunno.

GROS GAS:
Hey, Fred, use the head, okay?

FRED:
There's Murray. Hi, Murray. Sorry we're late.

MURRAY:
That's okay. Hi, guys. Sit down.

GROS GAS:
Hey, Claude, donne-moi six draft.

CLAUDE:
Six?

GROS GAS:
You want two beer, Murray?

MURRAY:
    No, I'm back on my diet.

GROS GAS:
    Okay, quatre.

FRED:
    I only want one beer.

GROS GAS:
    Okay, so I'll drink three.

CLAUDE:
    Three?

GROS GAS: *holding up four fingers*
    Non, quatre.

CLAUDE:
    Okay, quatre.

    He exits to the other side of the tavern.

FRED:
    I don't think it's gonna work, Gas.

GROS GAS:
    Hey, Fred.

FRED:
    How's it gonna work?

GROS GAS:
    Hey, why not?

FRED:
    You tell me.

GROS GAS:
    We just do it, that's all.

FRED:

> Look, what about the guys in 101 and the office workers, eh? What are we gonna do about them?

GROS GAS:

> You're not listening to me.

FRED:

> Look, I just don't think it's gonna work.

MURRAY:

> Hey, you guys. You wanna let me in on this?

GROS GAS:

> They get me, they get you too, Fred. That's all.

FRED:

> What do you mean by that?

GROS GAS:

> Just what I say.

FRED:

> Look, Gas, I don't need this kind of shit.

MURRAY:

> Hey, relax.

FRED:

> He's calling me a suck.

GROS GAS:

> I don't call you suck. I call you chicken.

FRED:

> Yeah, well, cluck, cluck, cluck.

GROS GAS:

> Yeah, cluck, cluck, cluck.

MURRAY:
>Relax. Not so loud.

GROS GAS:
>That's easy for you, eh, Murray? Relax, relax.

MURRAY:
>Hey, have a heart. I was up late last night, okay?

GROS GAS:
>Poor Murray.

MURRAY:
>So, what's happening, huh? Fred, what's happening?

FRED:
>Well, I figured I'd phone ya, Murray. Hope you don't mind me calling your house, but, uh, your office line is always busy, eh?

MURRAY:
>Sure, Fred, so, uh . . .

GROS GAS:
>I want to walk out.

FRED:
>He wants to walk out.

MURRAY:
>You want to walk out, huh? Why?

GROS GAS:
>Because I need a holiday, okay?

MURRAY:
>The new foreman's been hassling ya, huh?

FRED:
>Yeah, he's been on our backs.

GROS GAS:

Hey, guess who gets all the shift work and all the heavy loads, eh? And last week there . . . Hey, remember last week . . . They lost our cheques. Five days, Murray, we wait for our cheques.

MURRAY:

So maybe they lost them.

GROS GAS:

Hey, just our cheques. Nobody else's? Fuck you, câlice!

FRED:

Anyhow, Murray, that's why I called ya.

GROS GAS:

And now they got that new guy down there on the dock, that new foreman there with the big fuckin' mouth.

FRED:

Hey, Gas, shh.

GROS GAS:

Thinks he's tough. Used to be a cop.

FRED:

Hey, Gas.

GROS GAS:

So, this guy, you know, Pacquette there, the big boss there in the office? Well, the foreman there, that's his brudder-in-law . . . beau frère.

MURRAY:

Brother-in-law, huh?

GROS GAS:

Yeah, the son of a bitch.

FRED:

    Hey, Gas, he's sitting right over there.

GROS GAS:

    What? You worried? I'm not worried. Fuck him!

FRED:

    Okay.

GROS GAS:

    Fuck him, okay?

FRED:

    Yeah, yeah.

MURRAY:

    It's that guy over there, huh?

FRED:

    Yeah.

GROS GAS:

    He's cute, eh?

MURRAY:

    Right, I think I'm getting the picture.

GROS GAS:

    They're out to get us, Murray.

FRED:

    Jean-Luc quit. So did old Bill Ryan.

MURRAY:

    So, how long has this been going on?

FRED:

    Since the last walkout.

GROS GAS:

    They want to get all the guys with guts.

MURRAY:

> Right. So, why didn't somebody call me? I mean, you got my number. You belong to a union now, right.

FRED:

> Well, that's true, Murray, but . . .

GROS GAS:

> Don't give me that shit, Murray.

MURRAY:

> You don't have my number?

GROS GAS:

> Yeah, sure, and I phone the office and "Hello," the girl says, "Who? Murray? Murray Friedman? I'm sorry, he's not in right now. Can I take a message?" Eh? Eh?

MURRAY:

> Okay, okay.

GROS GAS:

> Okay, so don't give me that shit.

> *He opens up his lunch bag and starts eating.*

MURRAY:

> Okay, so I've been busy. Somebody has to work on the spring contract.

GROS GAS:

> Busy, busy, busy.

MURRAY:

> Look, anyhow, we don't want to walk out unless we have to, right?

FRED:

> Right.

GROS GAS:
> Walk out, then we talk.

MURRAY:
> Hey, I understand you're mad, but first I have to go meet with Pacquette and the other managers. I mean, we got to know where they stand, right?

GROS GAS:
> We know where they stand. Right on top of us, câlice.

MURRAY:
> Look, lemme see what I can do. Let me talk to them first.

FRED:
> Yeah, do that, Murray. We got enough trouble without this.

GROS GAS:
> You better talk fast, Murray.

MURRAY:
> Hey, we'll probably be out on strike this April anyhow.

GROS GAS:
> Sure, when the company wants us to.

> *CLAUDE enters and starts putting beer down on MURRAY's table.*

FRED:
> You talk to Pacquette and Roman, Murray. We'll wait.

GROS GAS:
> Yeah, we're very good at that, hostie.

FRED:
>What else can we do?

GROS GAS:
>You scared, eh, Fred? They got you scared?

CLAUDE:
>Hey, hey, Gros Gas.

GROS GAS:
>Quoi?

CLAUDE:
>Pas manger ici. You know dat.

GROS GAS:
>Okay, okay. Put the beer there.

CLAUDE:
>That's the law.

CHABOUGAMOU: *echoing him*
>That's the law.

GROS GAS:
>Okay, okay. He's the new law here?

>*He points to CHABOUGAMOU.*

>The new boss?

FRED:
>Look, Gas, if we had a chance, any kind of chance.

GROS GAS:
>So, you want to wait for Murray, eh? Maudit Christ, you'll wait a long time.

CLAUDE:
>Hey, Gas, pas manger ici, okay?

GROS GAS: *swallowing his sandwich*
Okay, okay, reste tranquille, tabarnac! Look, fini, finished, no more, c'est toute, okay? Put the beer there.

CLAUDE:
C'est pas moi, c'est la boss.

CHABOUGAMOU:
Oui, la boss.

GROS GAS:
Yeah, yeah, the boss, okay.

GROS GAS pays CLAUDE and he moves away.

FOREMAN: *looking at GROS GAS*
Hey.

GROS GAS:
Quoi?

FOREMAN: *still looking at GROS GAS*
Claude, gimme some matches.

CLAUDE puts some matches down on the the FOREMAN's table and exits.

FRED:
Me, I'm already looking for another job.

GROS GAS:
Hey, Fred, it's all the same old shit. It don't matter where you go.

FRED:
I'm looking around.

MURRAY:
Hey, it's gonna be alright. Believe me.

GROS GAS:

> I want a meeting. Get all the guys together. Me, I'll talk to the frogs and you, Fred, you talk to the blokes just like last time. It's easy.

FRED:

> Yeah.

GROS GAS:

> Just do it.

FRED:

> Why bother me? Why don't ya get Jackie or Jean-Guy to do it?

GROS GAS:

> Because the guys know you, Fred. They trust you because you're such a dumb squarehead. Tête carrée.

FRED:

> Thanks a lot.

MURRAY:

> Look, just let me talk to Pacquette and Roman, okay?

> *The warehouse whistle blows.*

FRED:

> Well, that's it.

GROS GAS:

> I got this beer.

MURRAY:

> So, no meeting until I talk to the managers, right?

FRED:

> Right.

GROS GAS:

> Tell me one thing, Murray.

MURRAY:
> What?

GROS GAS:
> We always wait, they always win. Why is that? Eh?

MURRAY:
> I got the message, Gas. Ten-four, loud and clear.
> I got it.

GROS GAS:
> I hope so, câlice.

FOREMAN: *passing by MURRAY's table, on his way to the door* Hey.

FRED:
> Let's go.

GROS GAS:
> My beer.

FOREMAN: *at the door, shaking his keys*
Hey, hey, the whistle.

GROS GAS: *mimicking the FOREMAN*
Hey, hey, the beer.

FOREMAN: *still shaking his keys*
Come on. Come on.

GROS GAS:
> HEY, I'M NOT A DOG, TABARNAC!

> *He heads towards the FOREMAN, but is stopped by FRED and MURRAY.*

MURRAY:
> Hey, Gros Gas. Hey, alright. Hey, I'll vouch for him.
> We'll be right over. I'll vouch for him.

FOREMAN:
>Get to work.

MURRAY:
>Yeah, yeah.

FOREMAN:
>You do your job, okay?

MURRAY:
>Right, no problems.

>*The FOREMAN exits.*

>Wow! Hey, Gas, watch it.

GROS GAS:
>Aw, baise mon cul.

MURRAY:
>Be careful with that guy, Gas. I'm serious.

GROS GAS:
>Next time . . .

MURRAY:
>Next time, make sure you got witnesses, okay?
>Otherwise, you get no protection from the union,
>understand?

GROS GAS:
>I just want to drink my beer.

MURRAY:
>Drink your beer.

CLAUDE:
>Hey, I don't want no trouble here, eh?

MURRAY:
>No trouble.

FRED:
>Let's go.

MURRAY:
>Okay, so no meeting until you hear from me, right?
>Gros Gas?

GROS GAS:
>I just want to . . .

MURRAY:
>. . . drink your beer, right?

GROS GAS:
>Oui.

FRED:
>I'll see you guys over there.

MURRAY:
>Hold it, Fred. Here.

>*He hands FRED a beer.*

FRED:
>My truck's at the dock.

MURRAY:
>Drink it or we'll never get him out of here.

FRED:
>Shit! La merde!

CHABOUGAMOU: *singing*
>Please release me, let me go.
>I don't love you anymore . . .

GROS GAS:
>Ferme ta gueule, toi.

CHABOUGAMOU:

Hey, you know that one, eh? You know that one.

*GROS GAS leans over and gives CHABOU-
GAMOU a beer.*

MURRAY:

Fred, talk to Gros Gas, okay? Slow him down.

FRED:

What do ya think I've been doing?

MURRAY:

Yeah, I know you're doing your best.

FRED:

The guys are mad, Murray. Real mad, and I don't
blame them.

MURRAY:

Yeah, I know.

FRED:

You gotta come around more often, Murray. Maybe
this wouldn't happen.

MURRAY:

Okay, okay, but talk to him, alright?

JACKIE and FRANK enter.

FRANK:

Cool it, Jackie. Cool it.

JACKIE:

Yeah, well, he can shove his fuckin' invoice up his
fuckin' ass, man.

FRANK:

Ya gonna leave the truck there?

JACKIE:
    Fuckin' right.

FRANK:
    It's gonna block up the dock.

GROS GAS:
    Hey, Jacques.

JACKIE: *sitting down at a table*
    He wants me to wait, I'll fuckin' wait.

FRANK:
    Yeah, but, uh, Jackie . . .

GROS GAS:
    Hey, Jacques. Hey, bon homme.

He goes over to JACKIE's table.

JACKIE:
    Don't fuckin' bon homme me, man.

GROS GAS:
    We're gonna have a meeting.

JACKIE:
    Yeah, goody gumdrops. Hey, Claude.

GROS GAS:
    We're gonna vote out the foreman.

JACKIE:
    Vote him out? I'm gonna fuckin' punch him out.
    Where's Claude?

MURRAY:
    Hi, Jackie.

JACKIE:
    Next time he's gonna get a taste, man.

MURRAY:
>What's wrong?

GROS GAS:
>Hey, Jacques. You talk to the squareheads, I'll talk
>to the frogs.

JACKIE:
>You gonna serve ice cream?

GROS GAS:
>Hey, Jacques.

JACKIE:
>Later, Gas.

MURRAY:
>Jackie, I'm gonna talk to George Roman about that
>new foreman right now. I'll see you later, okay?
>You'll be here?

JACKIE:
>Yeah, yeah.

GROS GAS:
>Jacques.

MURRAY:
>Come on, Gas, come on.

FRED: *handing FRANK a beer*
>Here, Frank. Have a beer.

FRANK:
>Oh, thanks, Fred.

>>*MURRAY, FRED and GROS GAS exit. GROS
>>GAS has a glass of beer with him.*

CLAUDE:
>Hey, Gas, put it back. Put it back.

GROS GAS gulps down the beer and hands the glass to CLAUDE.

JACKIE:
Hey, Claude, four beers.

FRANK:
Four?

CLAUDE:
Four.

JACKIE: *holding up four fingers*
Yeah, four.

CLAUDE:
Quatre.

He exits to get the beer.

CHABOUGAMOU:
Deux. Hey, deux, Claude.

JACKIE:
It's too fuckin' much, man.

FRANK:
Aw, the foreman's a goof. Forget it.

JACKIE:
Bring the invoice to the office. Fuck him!

FRANK:
Look, he wants to pick a fight with ya.

JACKIE:
Good, I'm ready.

FRANK:
Hey, I dunno. Look what he did to Ti-Jean. He's bad news, that guy.

JACKIE:
> Yeah, well, I'll just get a gun and shoot the fucker.

FRANK: *handing JACKIE his glass of beer*
> Yeah, yeah. Here, you want the rest?

> *JACKIE gulps down the beer.*

JACKIE:
> Shit, man.

FRANK:
> Aw, count to a hundred, you'll relax.

JACKIE:
> Eh?

FRANK:
> A hundred. You know, one, two, three, four . . .

JACKIE:
> Fuck off, Frank!

> *JERRY goes over to JACKIE's table. He has his sunglasses on.*

JERRY:
> Hey, man, got a light?

JACKIE:
> Eh? Give the goof a light.

FRANK:
> Hey, that's Jerry Nines.

JERRY:
> Say, Jackie, what's happening?

JACKIE:
> Nines? That you, Jerry?

JERRY: *taking off his sunglasses*
Yeah, it's me.

JACKIE:
Wow! Hey, fuck!

JERRY:
Hey, man.

JACKIE:
Hey, what you doing here? Hey.

JERRY:
I came down to see ya.

They hug.

JACKIE:
Hey, fuck! Shit! La merde!

JERRY:
Good to see your face, man.

JACKIE:
Yeah, still alive.

JERRY:
Yeah, me too. So, uh, what's with the monkey suit, eh?

JACKIE:
Aw, I'm a squarejohn now.

JERRY:
Squarejohn, eh? Jumping Jack Robinson goes straight.

JACKIE:
Yeah, well . . .

JERRY:
Hey, only kidding ya, man. Hi, Frank.

JACKIE:
Yeah, hey, Frank, it's Jerry.

FRANK:
Hey, so you're getting famous, eh?

JERRY shakes hands with FRANK.

JERRY:
Yeah, say, Frank, what's happening, eh?

FRANK:
Aw, ya know.

JERRY:
Still winning at pool?

FRANK:
Yeah, you wanna play?

JACKIE:
Claude. Hey, Claude.

JERRY:
So, what's it been, man? Three or four years?

JACKIE:
Too long, man.

JERRY:
Yeah.

JACKIE:
Hey, Claude.

CLAUDE: *sticking his head around the corner*
Quoi?

JACKIE:
Make that ten beers.

CLAUDE:
    Ten? Dix?

FRANK:
    Ten beers. Hey, Jackie, on our lunch?

JACKIE:
    Yeah, ten.

CHABOUGAMOU:
    Deux, Claude. Hey, deux.

FRANK:
    I hope you're thirsty, Jerry.

JERRY:
    Yeah, hey, so, uh, what's new? New York, New
    Jersey, New Brunswick.

JACKIE:
    New Helsinki, New Tokyo.

JERRY:
    Yeah.

JACKIE:
    You look tired, man.

JERRY:
    Aw, was up late last night.

JACKIE:
    Still with Linda?

JERRY:
    Yeah, yeah.

JACKIE:
    How is she?

JERRY:
> Fine. Hey, I dropped by your place. Irene told me you'd be here.

JACKIE:
> Oh, yeah?

JERRY:
> She's looking good. The kid too.

JACKIE:
> Ya seen Sean, eh?

JERRY:
> Yeah, got a dumb Mick face just like his old man.

JACKIE:
> Cute, eh?

JERRY:
> All freckles and ears. Irene's looking good.

JACKIE:
> Aw, got her hair cut . . . makes her look like a housewife.

JERRY:
> A nice flat there, man.

JACKIE:
> Had a big fight with her about that . . . said her hair gets in the way.

JERRY:
> I really missed Montreal, man. It's good to be back.

FRANK:
> Hey, so you're famous now, eh? TV, radio, newspapers . . . big time.

JERRY:
Yeah, I'm a star of the silver screen. Yeah.

JACKIE:
Yeah, so how're the books doing and the play?

FRANK:
Heard the play was a big hit.

JERRY:
Yeah, it's doing alright. Yeah.

FRANK:
Making money, eh?

JERRY:
Yeah, bits and pieces. Yeah.

FRANK:
The good life.

JERRY:
Beats working in a factory, man.

JACKIE:
Anything beats that, man.

JERRY:
Yeah, well, you know, I'm, uh, making a living doing something I like and that's about the best you can get.

FRANK:
Hey, I seen you in an interview on TV.

JERRY:
Oh, yeah?

FRANK:

> Fuckin' funny or what? Did ya see it, Jackie? There's the interviewer asking all these questions and there's Jerry sitting there all slouched over. Uh, yeah, uh, no, uh, I dunno . . . ask me another question.

> *FRANK and JACKIE laugh.*

JERRY:

> Yeah, doing my wooden Indian act.

FRANK:

> Fuckin' funny or what?

JACKIE:

> Yeah, well try talking next time, ya know?

FRANK:

> Yeah, you're the only celebrity we got from the Point, so, uh, smarten up.

JACKIE:

> Yeah.

JERRY:

> Aw, fuckin' CBC hacks, man, in their leather safari suits. They're all goofs, man. Can't talk to goofs.

JACKIE:

> Anyhow, we're proud of ya, man. I mean, I didn't take ya seriously when you started those journals years ago, man, but, uh, ya did it . . .

FRANK:

> Yeah, I read your book. Well, most of it . . . It's good.

JERRY:

> Thanks.

JACKIE:

> Ya put Point Saint Charles on the map, man.

42

JERRY:
Well, I tried.

FRANK:
Yeah, but don't let it go to your head.

JERRY:
Don't worry, it stays on the map.

FRANK:
Ya sure?

JERRY:
What do ya mean?

FRANK:
Well, my brudder saw ya uptown last week wearing sunglasses.

JERRY:
Yeah, so?

FRANK:
So, it was twelve o'clock midnight, eh?

JERRY:
Yeah, so? I like sunglasses.

FRANK:
Ya sure it's not going to your head? I mean, stuff like that sneaks up on ya. Like, uh, I seen this guy in a movie once. He had sunglasses, right, and . . .

JACKIE:
This isn't a movie, Frank.

FRANK:
Yeah, I know, but this guy, he . . .

JACKIE:
Okay, Frank.

FRANK:
Okay, what?

JACKIE:
Just okay, okay?

FRANK:
Okay.

JERRY:
Got a short fuse this morning, eh?

JACKIE:
He don't know when to stop, man.

FRANK:
What do ya mean, stop? Look, I stopped.

JACKIE: *controlling himself*
Frank . . .

FRANK:
Okay.

JERRY:
Hey, uh, did ya read my book, Jackie?

JACKIE:
Yeah, I read it. You were hard on me, man.

JERRY:
Yeah, I was worried about that.

JACKIE:
Like, I'm not denying it all happened, man, but wow,
fuck! I mean, uh, like I come across like the kiss of
death, man.

JERRY:
Too heavy, eh?

44

JACKIE:
> Well, fuck, what do ya expect, man?

JERRY:
> Well, that was years ago, man. I mean, you were
> living in basements and shooting speed, man.
> I figured it was hepatitis for ya, game over . . .

JACKIE:
> Yeah.

JERRY:
> Like, uh, I was just writing what I thought was true
> at the time. Hey, come on, Jackie. Didn't mean to put
> ya down, man. You know that.

JACKIE:
> Yeah, okay, but do me a favour, alright?

JERRY:
> Yeah.

JACKIE:
> Don't spell my name with a "y," okay? Spell it with
> an "i-e." J-a-c-k-i-e. Jackie, not Jacky. I mean, why
> "y," man?

JERRY:
> I liked it with "y."

JACKIE:
> Makes me embarrassed, like I'm a dummy or
> something. D-u-m-m-y, dummy.

> *CLAUDE enters.*

JERRY:
> Okay, "i-e."

JACKIE:
> I mean, why "y," man?

JERRY:
Got ya, J-a-c-k-i-e, Jackie.

JACKIE:
Try it, you'll like it.

JERRY:
Yeah, I'll like it.

CLAUDE: *putting ten beers down on the table*
Trois et cinquante.

FRANK:
I don't believe this.

JERRY: *digging into his pocket*
I'll get it.

JACKIE:
Naw, you get the next one.

JACKIE pays CLAUDE for the beer.

FRANK:
Hey, Claude, we got a celebrity here today.

CLAUDE:
Ah, oui?

FRANK:
Yeah, Jerry here. He's famous.

CLAUDE:
Ah, oui? You play hockey, you?

JACKIE:
Yeah, Claude. Philadelphia Flyers.

CLAUDE:
Good.

FRANK:
   Naw, he wrote a play, Claude. A play.

CLAUDE: *shrugging*
   Ah, oui. Good.

   CLAUDE goes over to CHABOUGAMOU.

FRANK:
   Ya hafta be in a beer commercial before Claude knew
   you were famous.

CLAUDE: *shaking CHABOUGAMOU awake*
   Hey, hey, lève-toi, lève-toi. You want to sleep, you go
   home.

CHABOUGAMOU:
   Quoi? Quoi? Hey, Claude, deux bières. Deux bières,
   Claude.

   *CLAUDE moves away from CHABOUGAMOU
   and exits.*

FRANK:
   Hey, Chabougamou, who won the war, eh? Who won
   the war?

CHABOUGAMOU:
   The war? Hey, Claude. Claude, attend peu. Une bière.

JERRY: *bringing a beer over to CHABOUGAMOU*
   Hey, une bière. Reste tranquille, okay?

CHABOUGAMOU:
   Hey, I speak the English, me.

JERRY:
   Oh, yeah? Me too.

FRANK: *opening his old lunch box*
   Now you got a friend for life, Jerry.

47

JERRY: *coming back to JACKIE's table and tapping FRANK's lunch box* Hey, what's this? Family heirloom or something?

FRANK:
Belonged to my old man. Dominion Coal and Steel.

JACKIE: *opening his lunch bag*
Wanna sandwich? Egg?

JERRY:
Egg? Aw, okay.

JACKIE:
Real squarejohn, eh?

JERRY:
Aw, fuck, man. It beats hepatitis.

JACKIE:
I don't know about that.

JERRY:
Ya been here three years, eh?

JACKIE:
Yeah, Frankie here got me the job.

JERRY:
Three years, wow! That's all-time record, eh?

JACKIE:
Yeah, well, shit's up to here now.

JERRY:
Hassles?

FRANK:
Fuckin' shift work. Overtime all the time.

JACKIE:
　　French and English, office and warehouse. The
　　company's got us all fucked up, man.

FRANK:
　　Push, push, push, all the fuckin' time.

JACKIE:
　　It's the French guys on the move now, man. They're
　　the ones kicking shit.

FRANK:
　　Yeah, they don't believe in the Pope no more.

JERRY:
　　Yeah, right.

JACKIE:
　　Ya still into politics?

JERRY:
　　Me? Yeah.

JACKIE:
　　Marxism?

JERRY:
　　Yeah, workers of the world please unite. Yours truly,
　　Jerry Nines.

JACKIE:
　　Hey, I want you to meet Murray. He's the guy I talk
　　politics to since ya left.

JERRY:
　　Oh, yeah?

FRANK: *opening his sandwich wrapper*
　　Oh, no, not baloney again!

JACKIE:

> College guy. Worked here as a releaser, then got a job in the new union.

JERRY:

> College kid radical, eh?

FRANK:

> Fuckin' baloney! No mustard either!

JACKIE:

> He's got a B.A., but that don't get ya jobs no more.

JERRY:

> Better off without a B.A.

JACKIE:

> Yeah, makes me glad they threw me outta Grade 8.

FRANK:

> Fuck, this is the third time this week I got baloney!

JACKIE:

> Hey, so tell your mudder to make ya something different.

FRANK:

> Can't do that.

JACKIE:

> Why not?

FRANK:

> I make them myself.

JACKIE:

> He makes them himself. Fuck, I've known plant life smarter than you, Frank.

FRANK:

> Va fanculo!

JACKIE:
Hey, where's Claude? I ordered ten beers, not eight.
Hey, Claude.

FRANK:
We got time for all that beer?

JACKIE:
All the time in the world, man.

FRANK:
What about the truck?

JACKIE:
Look, the foreman told us to wait, so we'll fuckin'
wait.

FRANK:
We got forty minutes.

JACKIE:
Don't worry about it, Frank.

FRANK: *looking at his watch*
Thirty-nine.

JERRY:
Hey, that new foreman looks like bad news, eh? The
bald guy.

FRANK:
Yeah, used to be a cop. Now he thinks he's Kojak.

JACKIE:
Only one thing worse than a cop and that's an ex-cop

FRANK:
Jackie's the only guy that talks back to him.

JACKIE:
Gros Gas ain't afraid of him.

FRANK:
> Gros Gas is too stupid to be afraid of him.

JACKIE:
> He's too stupid, eh?

FRANK:
> Yeah.

JACKIE:
> And I'm too stupid too, eh? Eh?

> *He shoves FRANK.*

FRANK:
> Hey, man, what's with you?

JACKIE: *getting up from the table and exiting to the washroom* You're getting on my nerves, Frank. I'm going for a piss.

FRANK:
> Hey, I didn't say he was stupid, did I? I mean, sometimes he gets a little dingy, but, uh . . .

JERRY:
> Really short fuse, eh?

FRANK:
> Drinking too much, man. Never could hold the booze.

JERRY:
> Yeah, Irene's really worried. I wanna talk to him.

FRANK:
> Yeah, do that, Jerry. He'll listen to you, I think.

JERRY:
> What's with him anyhow?

FRANK:
> Aw, work's getting him down. He's been getting right strange lately.

JERRY:
> Bad, eh?

FRANK:
> Yeah, you talk to him, Jerry.

JERRY:
> Well, hope I can say the right thing, ya know?

FRANK:
> Yeah, well, you know Jackie. It's not what you say, it's how ya say it.

JERRY:
> Yeah, right.

FRANK:
> I mean, you could tell him to eat shit, if ya just say it the right way, like, uh . . .

> *He speaks sweetly.*

> Hi, Jackie. Eat shit, ya know? Don't listen to the words. It's the tone.

JERRY:
> Yeah.

FRANK:
> The tone of voice.

JERRY:
> Yeah, gotta get the tone right.

> *The telephone rings and CLAUDE enters and answers it.*

FRANK hides his food.

CLAUDE:
Allô, Charlie's Tavern? Murray? Murray Friedman?
Is Murray here?

FRANK:
No.

CLAUDE:
Non.

CLAUDE hangs up the telephone.

JACKIE re-enters from the washroom.

JACKIE:
Hey, Claude.

CLAUDE:
Oui?

JACKIE:
I asked for ten beers, not eight.

CLAUDE:
You want two more?

JACKIE:
No, four more.

FRANK:
Four more? Hey, Jackie, have a heart. Make that one
beer with three straws.

CHABOUGAMOU: *holding up two fingers*
Deux, Claude. Hey, Claude.

CLAUDE:
Non, pas bière pour toi.

CHABOUGAMOU:
Hey, I pay you tomorrow, Claude. Next week? Deux,
Claude.

FRANK: *holding up two fingers, making the Peace sign*
Peace. Peace, eh?

JACKIE:
Give him a beer, Claude, or he's gonna start stealing
ours.

CHABOUGAMOU:
Oui, give him a beer, that's right.

CLAUDE:
No beer for him. He piss himself, then I have to
throw him out.

He exits.

CHABOUGAMOU:
Hey, Claude. Claude, attend peu, Claude.

JACKIE:
Hey, Ti-Cul. Ferme ta gueule, toi.

CHABOUGAMOU:
Hey, I speak the English, me.

FRANK:
Some people got cats and dogs for pets. Claude's got
a drunk.

JERRY:
Yeah.

FRANK:
Claude's been in the Navy. Navy guys are weird, man.
They get like philosophers, ya know?

JACKIE:
>He's a fuckin' artist too, man. Ever see him bounce drunks outta this place? Hey, poetry in motion, man. Not one wasted move.

FRANK:
>Shoulda seen him bounce Newfie outta here last week. Did a ricochet on him, twice off the table, once off the wall and . . . boom . . . a hole in one.

JACKIE:
>Yeah, great moments in sports.

JERRY:
>Hey, don't tell me old Newfie's still around, eh?

JACKIE:
>Oh, yeah, got off the Toronto bus for a drink and never found his way back.

FRANK:
>Yeah, Newfie's still haunting the taverns.

CHABOUGAMOU:
>Newfie, Newfie, pas bon. Dat guy, he takes my beer. No good.

FRANK:
>Chabougamou hates Newfie.

CHABOUGAMOU:
>No good, dat guy.

FRANK:
>No class, eh?

JACKIE:
>Only room for one drunk in this tavern.

JERRY: *lifting his glass*
>Well, here's to us, man. The survivors.

FRANK:
> Si, down the hatch, amigos.

JACKIE:
> He's a fuckin' Mexican now.

FRANK:
> Yeah, I mean, uh, this reminds me of a flick I seen.
> Old friend meets friends in tavern, right? . . . *The
> Return of the Magnificent Seven* or something. Yul
> Brynner. Did ya see it, Jackie?

JACKIE:
> Later, Frank.

JERRY:
> Yeah, so I'm back, man.

JACKIE:
> Back for good?

JERRY:
> Yeah, I think so.

JACKIE:
> Toronto too much for ya?

JERRY:
> Hogtown, man.

FRANK:
> Hey, I got relatives there.

JACKIE:
> Fuckin' Wops got relatives everywhere.

FRANK:
> Yeah, we're gonna take over the world.

JERRY:
> Yeah, Toronto, man. Wow!

FRANK:
What's the money like there? Good or what?

JERRY:
Yeah, the money's good, but I had to quit, man. Too much business in show business.

JACKIE:
Too many games?

JERRY:
Too much competition, man. Like, it's insane. People fuckin', bouncing off the walls and all kinds of weird faggotty power trips going on, and me, I don't wanna win or lose, I don't wanna play. Fuck it!

JACKIE:
Yeah, right.

FRANK:
Sounds as bad as the warehouse.

JERRY:
It's worse, man. Like, you got to imagine this huge fuckin' pyramid and at the top you got the executives, right, and the administrators and the bureaucrats, and then the hacks and the friends of the hacks, and the friends of the friends and their friends, and then, there's us and we're treated like shit, man, especially actors. I wouldn't be an actor if ya paid me.

JACKIE:
Weird scenes in the gold mines, eh?

JERRY:
Yeah, CBC groupies, man. Guy I know calls them clusterfucks 'cause they hang in clusters and fuck each other.

JACKIE:
Clusterfucks. In the corners, in bunches.

FRANK:
>Like grapes.

JERRY:
>Really screwed up, man, and they're all into trippy
>things like group therapy and meditation and
>vegetation and houses in the country. Sitting
>around in circles fuckin' staring into each other's
>eyeballs.

JACKIE:
>Yeah, how you handling all that shit, man?

JERRY: *making juggling motions*
>Very carefully.

JACKIE:
>We'd hate to lose ya, Jerry. Most guys who leave the
>Point never look back.

JERRY:
>Yeah, but there's nowhere to go, man. I mean, who
>wants to grow up to be Richard Nixon, right? It's
>not worth it.

JACKIE:
>So what are ya gonna do?

JERRY:
>Me? I'm gonna get a flat and write books. No more
>show biz.

>*The telephone starts ringing.*

JACKIE:
>Can ya make a living doing that?

JERRY:
>I'm gonna try.

FRANK:
>
Ya oughta write skin books, Jerry, there's good
money in skin books. Get me a broad and I'll pose
for the cover, ha ha. . . .

> *CLAUDE enters with a tray of beer. He answers
the telephone.*

CLAUDE:
>
Allô, Charlie's Tavern? Who is this? This is Claude,
me. Who are you? I don't know you. Murray
Friedman again? Murray here?

FRANK:
>
No.

CLAUDE:
>
Non.

> *He hangs up the telephone and comes over to
JACKIE's table and puts six beers on it.*

>
Un, deux, trois, quatre, cinq, six. Bonne fête. Happy
birthday.

> *JERRY pays CLAUDE and he exits.*

FRANK:
>
Trade ya a baloney sandwich for an egg?

JACKIE:
>
Fuck off!

FRANK:
>
Okay, I'll eat it. So what are ya doing now, Jerry?

JERRY:
>
Me? I'm working on a book.

FRANK:
>
Am I in it?

JERRY:

    Not this one, but, uh, Jackie is . . .

JACKIE:

    Oh? What do ya say about me in this one?

JERRY:

    Aw, ya know, the usual stuff, suave, sophisticated, debonair.

JACKIE:

    Fuck you, Nines!

FRANK:

    So what's this one about?

JERRY:

    Point Saint Charles back in the early Sixties. I'm calling it "Balconville."

JACKIE:

    Good title.

JERRY:

    People drinking beer on their balconies in the heat. "Where ya going this summer?" "Balconville." "Yeah, me too." "Balconville."

FRANK:

    Miami Bench.

JACKIE:

    Yeah.

JERRY:

    I'm writing about that time you, me and Budsy got caught in that big Lincoln, remember? We wanted to go down to Florida.

JACKIE:

    Yeah, Florida.

61

FRANK:
Budsy?

JERRY:
Yeah, Budsy. Had a bad arm from polio. Bad wing there? Remember?

FRANK:
Oh, yeah, Budsy. Save the butt, Budsy.

JERRY:
Yeah, Jackie had this thing about Florida. Somewhere over the rainbow there were girls with tits like watermelons.

FRANK:
Everybody was always running away in those days.

JERRY:
Nothing else to do.

JACKIE:
Ya'd phone somebody up and "Hullo? Is Joey dere?" "No, he just ran away. Call back next week."

FRANK:
Feet, do your thing.

JERRY:
We didn't know what was wrong, but we sure knew we didn't like it.

JACKIE:
Yeah.

FRANK:
Hey, back then I had to go uptown to get fucked. Grab a tit in the Point and ding-dong, the wedding bells start to ring.

JACKIE:

> Yeah, no fuckin' pill and next thing ya know your
> girl's pregnant and congratulations, you're on welfare
> pushing a baby carriage to the laundromat. Happened
> to my brudder.

FRANK:

> And everybody was afraid of The Bomb, remember?
> The Bomb?

JERRY:

> Yeah, The Bomb. I near forgot that.

FRANK:

> Sure, the teachers giving out pamphlets on what to
> do in case of nuclear attack.

JACKIE:

> Yeah, Number One: Duck.

ALL: *together*

> Number Two: Bend Over. Number Three: Kiss Your
> Ass Goodbye.

FRANK:

> Hey, no joke. My mudder got fuckin' neurotic over
> The Bomb, nightmares all the time, running scared
> into the house every time she saw a plane, fighting
> with the old man to get a basement flat . . . Crazy!

JACKIE:

> Yeah, The Bomb.

JERRY:

> Hey, what's been happening with Budsy? Seen him
> around?

JACKIE:

> They got him locked up . . . Yeah, he's been in the
> nuthouse the last couple of years.

JERRY:

> Oh, yeah? Got more spaced out or what?

JACKIE:

> Yeah.

JERRY:

> Shit, I'll have to go see him.

JACKIE:

> Aw, don't bother, man. Like, I used to go see him,
> talk to him while he watched TV, but after a while,
> man, I realized he was just watching TV, ya know?
> Sitting there with all those other zombies, man, his
> stomach all bloated from medication. Gone, man,
> faded out. Don't go.

JERRY:

> What a drag.

FRANK:

> Good thing they invented television.

JERRY:

> Yeah, and tranquillizers.

JACKIE:

> Budsy, Doulgie, Jean-Yves, all those guys we knew on
> the streets, man, fuckin' gone dead, crazy or in jail.

FRANK:

> Or working.

JERRY:

> Yeah, we lost a lot of good people.

FRANK:

> I never thought Jackie'd live to be eighteen, let alone
> twenty-eight.

64

JACKIE:
   Yeah, fuck, I feel like an ancestor.

JERRY:
   Yeah, well, that's the whole trip, man. I mean, guys
   like us were meant to wipe-out, self-destruct, 'cause
   there's no room for us. We don't fit in. That's what
   the Sixties were all about, man. People like us trying
   to stay alive.

JACKIE:
   Yeah, well, we sure kicked shit, eh?

FRANK:
   Yeah, it was fun.

JERRY:
   Aw, it was more than fun, man. The Sixties was a
   cultural revolution, man. China's got nothing on us.

JACKIE:
   Well, the streets are dead now, man. Nothing's
   happening. There's no scene.

JERRY:
   Not for long.

FRANK:
   Yeah, it's all disco and unisex now. Fuckin' mod
   faggots!

JACKIE:
   Yeah, no more "Satisfaction," man, now it's "Help
   Me Make It Through the Night." It's gone, man.
   The spirit's gone.

JERRY:
   No, it's just getting deeper.

JACKIE:

Deeper? Hey, all that crazy screaming and fighting back then, man, what good did it do us? It's still the same old game.

JERRY:

Yeah, still the same old game, but nobody believes in it anymore and that's the one big difference, man. Nobody believes in this bullshit anymore.

JACKIE:

I don't know.

JERRY:

The heads have changed, man. Blacks are proud, man. The French are proud. Women are proud. These people, they ain't ashamed of themselves anymore. That shit's gone, man. It's gone.

JACKIE:

Yeah, maybe.

FRANK:

Well, my life's still the same, still belongs to Sunny-brook's right here.

He points to the Sunnybrook's badge on his uniform.

JACKIE:

Yeah, squarejohn Frank here.

CHABOUGAMOU: *singing and waving his hands around like a conductor* Quand le soleil dit bonjour aux montagnes . . .

JACKIE:

Holy fuck!

FRANK:

Check Chabougamou over there with the orchestra.

JACKIE:
>   Hey, Chabougamou.

FRANK:
>   Change the record.

JERRY:
>   Shit, he'd make a fortune in the CBC, Québec
>   Spectacle.

FRANK:
>   Chabougamou Superspecial.

JACKIE: *whistling*
>   Hey, Ti-Cul. We heard that one.

CHABOUGAMOU:
>   Quoi?

JACKIE:
>   Quoi?

CHABOUGAMOU:
>   Quoi, quoi?

JACKIE:
>   Quoi, quoi, quoi? What are ya? A fuckin' duck?

CHABOUGAMOU:
>   Hey, don't press my nerve.

>   *He goes over to their table.*

FRANK:
>   He's coming over.

CHABOUGAMOU:
>   Smart guys, I know you.

JACKIE:
>   Ya do, eh?

CHABOUGAMOU:
>Me, I'm not from Chabougamou. Me, I know you.

JACKIE:
>Chabougamou, eh? That's right next to Point-aux-Pick and St-Louis de Ha-Ha.

CHABOUGAMOU:
>I know you, smart guy.

>*He tries to take a beer from their table.*

FRANK:
>Hey, touche pas. Touche pas, eh?

>*He grabs back the beer.*

CHABOUGAMOU:
>I pay you tomorrow.

FRANK:
>Yeah, sure.

CHABOUGAMOU:
>That's for sure, I pay you. Hey, me, I was in the Navy too, eh? The Navy, me.

FRANK:
>Yeah, sure, they musta used you for target practice. Hey, touche pas, okay?

>*He stops CHABOUGAMOU from taking another beer.*

CHABOUGAMOU: *taking out some papers and a photo from his wallet* Hey, me. I show you, me. Look, moi. C'est moi.

>*He drops the papers and the photo all over the table.*

JERRY:
> Yeah, yeah.

CHABOUGAMOU:
> Oui, that's me. Eh, regarde.

JERRY: *looking at his papers and the photo*
> Nice.

JACKIE:
> Hey, fuck off!

> *He pushes CHABOUGAMOU away.*
> *CHABOUGAMOU falls down.*

CHABOUGAMOU:
> Hey.

FRANK:
> Cha-boug-a-mou, eh?

CHABOUGAMOU:
> Maudit tête carrée bloke, hostie, tabarnac!

JACKIE:
> Hey, watch the language. Watch the language.

CHABOUGAMOU:
> C'est pas drole. Pas drole. Not funny, not funny at all.

CLAUDE: *entering*
> Hey, qu'est que tu fais?

CHABOUGAMOU:
> Pas drole.

CLAUDE: *yanking CHABOUGAMOU to his feet*
> Hey, out! Va-t-en! No sleeping on the floor.

CHABOUGAMOU:
Hey, Claude, non, non.

He hangs onto CLAUDE. CLAUDE drags him to the door and bounces him out.

CLAUDE:
Take some fresh air, tabarwit!

FRANK: *to JERRY*
He's good, eh?

JERRY:
Yeah.

CLAUDE: *passing by their table*
Maudit Christ!

FRANK:
Hey, Claude, I think he's part octopus.

CLAUDE: *exiting*
That's for sure, tabarnac!

JERRY:
Hey, he left all his stuff here.

FRANK:
Aw, don't worry. He'll be back.

CHABOUGAMOU enters grumbling.

Told ya he'd be back.

CHABOUGAMOU:
Maudit, tabarnac! Not funny, not funny at all.

JERRY: *bringing him his wallet and a glass of beer*
Hey, mon vieux. There ya go.

CHABOUGAMOU:
> Big car, me.

JERRY:
> Yeah, big car.

> *He goes back to his table.*

CHABOUGAMOU: *going around to all the tables collecting cigarette butts* Next time, maudit! Next time, c'est tout.

FRANK: *taking a big cigarette butt out of an ashtray and throwing it over to CHABOUGAMOU* Hey, Chabougamou, here's a nice big fat one.

> *The warehouse whistle blows. FRANK looks at his watch.*

> Well, it's about time. Fuck, look at all this beer. Come on, you guys, drink up.

JACKIE:
> No rush.

FRANK:
> Yeah, but the truck. It must be blocking up the dock by now.

JACKIE:
> Look, what did the foreman say this morning?

FRANK:
> He said wait.

JACKIE:
> So we'll wait.

FRANK:
> Yeah, but Jackie, the truck . . .

JACKIE:
> Have a beer, Frankie.

JERRY:
> Maybe I should meet ya later, Jackie.

JACKIE:
> Don't sweat it, man.

FRED: *entering*
> Hey, didn't you guys hear the whistle?

FRANK:
> Hi, Fred.

FRED:
> Hey, what the hell are you guys doing?

JACKIE:
> Listening to you, Fred.

FRED:
> Yeah, well, my truck's right behind yours, eh? I'm waiting for ya.

JACKIE:
> Relax.

FRED:
> Relax, yeah. Hurry up, eh?

> *He exits to the sound of beeping horns.*

FRANK:
> Hey, sounds real bad out there. I think I'm gonna check it out.

JACKIE:
> What about the beer?

FRANK:
> I'll be back.

JACKIE:
> When?

FRANK:
> Soon as I, uh, after I see. Look, ya know . . .

JACKIE:
> Fuck off, Frank!

FRANK:
> See ya, Jerry.

JERRY:
> See ya, Frank.

> *FRANK exits.*

JACKIE:
> Aw, fuck, come on, Jerry, let's play pool. You still as bad as you used to be?

JERRY:
> Yeah.

JACKIE:
> Okay, come on, I'll give ya a lesson.

> *He moves over to the pool table, puts a quarter into the slot and sets up the balls.*

JERRY:
> Look, uh, maybe I should meet you later, eh?

JACKIE:
> Why?

JERRY:
> Well, seems like a bad day to talk.

JACKIE:
> Nothing but bad days, man. You wanna break?

JERRY:
> No, go ahead . . . Straight life is rough on ya, eh?

JACKIE:
> Yeah . . . Been a long time, man.

> *They play as they talk.*

JERRY:
> Yeah, haven't played pool with you since, uh, Wellington Street.

JACKIE:
> That's right and ya still owe me two bucks.

JERRY:
> Fuck you! Hey, remember Louise?

JACKIE:
> Black Louise or French Louise?

JERRY:
> Rabbit Louise, the one there with the teeth.

JACKIE:
> Yeah, the teeth. She was a good pool player.

JERRY:
> She had the hots for ya, eh? Remember that night she caught ya down the alley there with Nicole?

JACKIE:
> Yeah, fuckin' hit me with a two-by-four. Good thing I got in that lucky punch.

JERRY:
> Yeah, Rabbit Louise.

JACKIE:

> She's dead, eh? Died in a car accident.

JERRY:

> Oh, yeah?

JACKIE:

> Yeah, her and Emile Gagnon in the same car.

JERRY:

> Aw, fuck, the both of them together, eh?

JACKIE:

> Yeah, you're right, man, we're survivors. There's not many of us left.

JERRY:

> Yeah, well, they got it planned that way.

> *FRED enters.*

FRED:

> There ya are. Hey, Jackie.

JACKIE:

> What?

FRED:

> There's four trucks out there stuck behind yours.

JACKIE:

> Oh, yeah? Good.

FRED:

> They're waiting for ya to unload, Jackie.

JACKIE:

> I'm busy.

FRED:

> Hey.

JACKIE:

> Your turn, Jerry.

FRED:

> Okay, look, give me the key so I can move your truck, okay?

JACKIE:

> Forget it, Fred.

FRED:

> Jackie, Frank's getting all kinds of shit out there.

JACKIE:

> Look, tell the foreman to come see me if he wants the truck moved, okay?

FRED:

> Tell him what?

JACKIE:

> Tell him I'm here, okay? No problem.

FRED:

> Jackie.

JACKIE:

> Your turn, Jerry.

FRED:

> Jackie.

JACKIE:

> Hey, Fred, stick around. Ya can play the winner.

FRED:

> Okay, it's your funeral.

> *He exits to the sound of beeping horns.*

JACKIE:
    Fuckin' squarejohns. They're pathetic, man.

JERRY:
    Sounds bad out there, man.

JACKIE:
    Music to my ears.

JERRY:
    Look, uh, why don't ya take a look out there, eh?

JACKIE:
    Forget it, man.

JERRY:
    Yeah, but, uh, just move the truck and come back.

    *JACKIE misses an easy shot and slams down his
    cue stick.*

JACKIE:
    Fuck, can't even play pool right no more.

JERRY:
    Hey, what's happening?

JACKIE:
    Hey, you like this monkey suit, eh? You want one?

JERRY:
    No.

    JACKIE sits down at a table.

JACKIE:
    Aw, ya got me on a bad day, man.

JERRY:
    Yeah.

JACKIE:

>Hey, I get on the bus every morning with my lunch
>bag and there's everybody else with their lunch bags
>and all of a sudden I know this is my life for the rest
>of my fuckin' life and I'm already sick of it.

JERRY:

>Yeah.

JACKIE:

>Irene gets her hair cut and me, I can't explain it, but
>feel my body getting stiff and slow like I'm becoming
>a truck driver, ya know? I don't like it, I don't like
>what's happening to me, man. Aw, shit, whose turn
>is it?

>*He gets up and heads back to the pool table.*

JERRY:

>Irene's worried about ya, man.

JACKIE:

>Yeah, well, I'm fuckin' worried too.

JERRY:

>She's scared, man. You're not gonna trip out on us,
>are ya?

JACKIE:

>I'm alright. Just drinking a bit.

JERRY:

>It's just changes, man. People change, times change.
>Just hang on.

JACKIE:

>Yeah, yeah. I know what to do, it's just doing it, ya
>know?

JERRY:

>Yeah, didn't mean to get heavy with ya.

JACKIE:
 I'm getting it together. It's just this straight life
 getting me down.

 The telephone starts to ring.

 Claude? Where's Claude?

 JACKIE goes over and answers the telephone.

 Yeah, hullo, Heartbreak Hotel? Murray Friedman?
 Never heard of him. Sunnybrook Farms? We don't
 want any.

 He hangs up the telephone.

 Fuckin' goofs got a voice like a typewriter.

 *The telephone starts ringing again. JACKIE
 picks up the receiver again.*

 Watch this. "Hold on." Hey, Chabougamou,
 Chabougamou, hey!

CHABOUGAMOU: *at his table, rolling cigarette butts*
 Quoi?

JACKIE: *pointing to the receiver*
 It's your wife.

CHABOUGAMOU:
 My wife? Which one?

JACKIE:
 Uh, the first one.

CHABOUGAMOU:
 The first one? Non.

JACKIE:
 Hey, it's the Mini-Loto. Yeah, Mini-Loto.

CHABOUGAMOU:
Mini-Loto.

JACKIE:
Yeah, oui.

CHABOUGAMOU gets to his feet.

CHABOUGAMOU:
Mini-Loto, moi?

JACKIE hands him the receiver.

JACKIE:
Oui.

*CHABOUGAMOU takes a crumpled Mini-Loto
ticket out of his pocket.*

CHABOUGAMOU:
Allô? Mini-Loto? C'est moi. The number . . . Allô?
The number, she's 746-825 . . . Allô? . . . 763. I win?
Allô? Eh, I win? Quoi? Quoi? Murray Friedman,
who? Quoi? The number, she's 746 . . . Allô? ALLO?
Hey, maybe I win? Hey, I want to pay for all the
beer. Hey, Claude. Hey, Claude.

JACKIE and JERRY laugh.

*CHABOUGAMOU drops the receiver and rushes
over to the other side of the tavern.*

CLAUDE: *offstage*
You again? Hey, out, out! Hey, câlice!

*CLAUDE enters and pushes CHABOUGAMOU
in front of him.*

CHABOUGAMOU:
Mini-Loto, Claude, Mini-Loto. I want to pay for all the
beer.

CLAUDE:
> Out, câlice! Don't come back.

> *He bounces CHABOUGAMOU out the door
> and puts the receiver back on the hook.*

> Dat guy, he's like a yoyo, tabarnac! Up and down,
> in and out.

> *JACKIE laughs and slaps five with JERRY.*

JACKIE:
> I don't believe it, man. Fuckin' showtime at
> Sunnybrook's.

JERRY:
> Yeah, man.

JACKIE:
> Yeah, hey, glad you're back, man. I missed ya.

JERRY:
> Missed you too, man.

JACKIE:
> Yeah, hey, we'll hafta put a party together, eh?

JERRY:
> Yeah, right.

JACKIE:
> How about Saturday night at my place?

JERRY:
> Saturday night. Yeah, okay, sure.

JACKIE:
> Hey, I'll phone up Jay, P.K., Toni. Get all the guys
> down.

JERRY:

    Yeah, right. Hey, how's Jimmy doing? Fast Jimmy, I'd like to see him again.

JACKIE:

    Yeah, I'll give him a call.

        FRANK and the FOREMAN enter with CHABOUGAMOU behind them.

FRANK:

    Jackie.

JACKIE:

    Here it comes.

JERRY:

    Shit!

FRANK:

    Jackie.

JACKIE:

    Hi, Frank.

FRANK:

    Jackie.

JACKIE:

    Relax.

FOREMAN:

    Hey, you! You!

JACKIE:

    Your turn, Jerry.

FOREMAN:

    Hey, come on! The truck, come on!

        He motions at JACKIE to leave.

JACKIE:
>You talking to me, man?

FOREMAN:
>Yeah, the truck. Come on!

JACKIE:
>I'm busy.

FOREMAN:
>Hey, this way, this way!

JACKIE: *mimicking the FOREMAN*
>This way, this way.

FOREMAN:
>You want trouble, you?

JACKIE:
>Look, man, this morning you told me to wait.

FOREMAN:
>I told you to bring the invoice down to the office
>first.

JACKIE:
>I never done that before.

FOREMAN:
>Yeah, well, you do it now.

JACKIE:
>Oh, yeah? Your turn, Jerry.

FOREMAN:
>Hey, goof!

>*He steps towards JACKIE. JACKIE turns
>around and lifts his cue stick.*

JACKIE:
> You want some, eh? You want some?

FOREMAN: *backing away*
> Hey, look, just phone the office, okay? Go ahead.

JACKIE:
> You phone them. I'm busy.

FOREMAN:
> Look, I'm trying to be a nice guy.

JACKIE:
> Fuck off, dipstick!

FOREMAN:
> You're brave in front of your friends, eh? Come on outside, outside, ya fuckin' lush.

> *The FOREMAN exits.*

> *JACKIE rushes out after the FOREMAN, followed by FRANK, JERRY and CLAUDE. The sounds of a fight are heard.*

> *During the fight, CHABOUGAMOU steals some beer and sits down, beaming, at his table.*

FRANK: *entering*
> Ya got him!

CLAUDE: *entering*
> Tabarnac!

JACKIE: *catching his breath as he enters, then looking at JERRY and grinning* I think I broke his nose.

FRANK:
> Ya got him good, Jackie.

JERRY:
    Better wash your face, man.

JACKIE:
    Eh?

JERRY:
    The face.

JACKIE:
    Eh? Yeah.

FRANK:
    Hey, the winner!

JACKIE:
    Hey.

    He exits to the washroom.

FRANK:
    Hey, man, he fuckin' did it. He's still good with that
    left, man. Boom!

JERRY:
    Yeah, still fuckin' crazy.

FRANK: *looking at their table*
    Hey, what happened to the beer? Hey, hey,
    Chabougamou.

    *He heads over to CHABOUGAMOU and grabs
    back the stolen beer.*

CHABOUGAMOU:
    Hey, c'est moi. C'est moi. Hey, Claude, hey.

CLAUDE: *pushing CHABOUGAMOU around*
    Hey, you want some beer, you pay. L'argent,
    tabarnac! L'argent.

CHABOUGAMOU:

    L'argent, l'argent, okay, okay, okay, l'argent.

    He exits.

FRANK:

    Hey, Claude, good fight, eh?

CLAUDE:

    Hey, this is no joke. That foreman there, he's got lots
    of friends.

FRANK:

    Not in this warehouse.

CLAUDE:

    Hey, dat guy, he's with the Boucher Brothers. You
    know the Bouchers? That's no joke.

FRANK:

    The Boucher Brothers. You sure?

CLAUDE:

    You don't believe me?

FRANK:

    Yeah, I believe ya, but, uh . . .

CLAUDE:

    Me, I don't know nutting, but this time, Jackie, he
    goes too far.

FRANK:

    Hey, you're not putting me on, eh?

CLAUDE:

    No joke. You drink up and you go, eh?

    He exits the other side of the tavern.

FRANK: *sitting down*
   Wow, man!

JERRY:
   The Boucher Brothers. That's the Saint Henri gang,
   eh? Always in the *Montréal Matin*?

FRANK:
   Yeah, they supply them with the bodies. Shit, and I
   just got my teeth fixed.

JERRY:
   Frank, we gotta get Jackie outta here.

FRANK:
   He's gonna wanna finish this beer.

JERRY:
   Okay, let's start drinking, man. The Bouchers, wow!

FRANK: *with a finger in his mouth*
   Fucker loosened one of my tooths. Wish I knew this
   was gonna happen. Wouldn't have gone to the dentist.

JERRY:
   Look, we'll try and coax him out, okay?

FRANK:
   Okay, we'll try.

JACKIE: *enters singing*
   Come on, baby, let the good times roll . . .

FRANK:
   Hey, ta-dum!

JERRY:
   Roll the drums.

JACKIE:
   Who's the champ? Who's the champ?

JERRY:
    You're the champ, man.

FRANK:
    A knockdown decision.

JACKIE:
    Fuckin' rough bastard.

    FRANK reaches to touch JACKIE's nose.

Don't touch, Frank.

FRANK:
    Just wanna see if the nose is . . .

JACKIE:
    It's alright.

JACKIE:
    Yeah, hey, musta kneed the fucker a hundred times
    and he's still on his feet. Fuckin' balls of steel.

JERRY:
    Quite the fight.

JACKIE: *putting a cold glass of beer against his eye*
    Hummm, that feels good.

FRANK:
    Well, the bad guys lost this time.

JACKIE:
    Yeah, I fuckin' enjoyed it, man.

FRANK:
    Good movie.

JACKIE:
    Wait till next week, Frankie, it gets even better.

JERRY:
> Yeah, well, let's drink up.

FRANK:
> Yeah.

JACKIE:
> Yeah, the fun has just begun. You getting the next round, Jerry?

JERRY:
> Uh, I figured we'd go over to your place.

JACKIE:
> Eh? Don't wanna go home now.

JERRY:
> Yeah, but your eye. Looks kinda funny.

JACKIE:
> It just looks bad.

JERRY:
> Well, uh, let's go over to my place. I gotta nice bottle of rum over there.

JACKIE:
> That sounds good.

JERRY:
> Yeah, Linda wants to see ya.

JACKIE:
> Sounds good, man.

FRANK:
> Yeah, give me the keys. I'll go move the truck.

JACKIE:
> Fuck the truck!

FRANK:
Yeah, but, uh . . . It's blocking up the dock.

JACKIE:
I don't wanna think about the truck right now, okay?
I'm relaxing.

FRANK:
Yeah, okay, uh . . . How long ya gonna relax?

JACKIE:
How the fuck do I know?

FRANK:
Well, uh . . . Why don't we go over and relax at
Jerry's place, eh?

JACKIE:
Look, what's happening?

FRANK:
Nothing, man.

JACKIE:
Don't shit me, Frank. What the fuck's happening?

FRANK:
The Boucher Brothers, that's what.

JERRY:
Aw, fuck, Frank!

JACKIE:
Boucher Brothers?

JERRY:
Christ, you got a big mouth, Frank.

FRANK:
Yeah, the Bouchers, man. The foreman's in tight with
them. Claude told us.

JACKIE:
>So you guys wanna move out?

JERRY:
>Yeah, I mean, the Bouchers.

JACKIE:
>Aw, look, they probably won't show anyhow.

FRANK:
>Yeah, well, I just got my teeth fixed, man.

JACKIE:
>Aw, come on, you guys, it's just like the bad old days, eh? Come on, Jerry, you're back in the Point now.

JERRY:
>I ain't been in a scrap for years, man.

JACKIE:
>Aw, listen, you got too much imagination.

JERRY:
>Yeah, imagination. Listen, let's finish this beer and go, okay?

FRANK: *getting up from the table and going over to the telephone* I'm gonna phone my mudder.

JACKIE:
>Everybody wants to go to heaven, but nobody wants to die.

FRANK: *on the telephone*
>Hullo, Ma! Yeah, it's me. Yeah. Nutting wrong. Yeah. Hey, ya know that insurance policy I got? Yeah, dat one. Are my teeth insured there too? My teeth. Yeah, just in case I have an accident or something. What?

JACKIE: *yelling*
>Hiya there, Mrs. Saladini.

FRANK:
>No, Ma, I'm not drinking with Jackie Robinson. I'm at work, Ma. At work, yeah. Ma, don't call me stupid. Ma. Ma?

>*He hangs up the telephone.*

>Shit, imagine your own mudder calling ya stupid.

>*He goes back to the table.*

JACKIE:
>Don't know why you're worried about yer teeth, Frank, the Bouchers'll probably kill ya anyway.

FRANK:
>Yeah. Ha ha, right?

JACKIE:
>Next time have your whole body insured.

>*CHABOUGAMOU enters and JACKIE, JERRY and FRANK jump.*

CHABOUGAMOU:
>Claude. Hey, Claude. Claude.

>*He exits the other side of the tavern carrying a tattered shopping bag full of empty soft drink bottles which rattle.*

JERRY:
>Hey, let's move from here. Go sit over there at the back.

JACKIE:
>Yeah, good idea.

FRANK:
>   Yeah, I wanna keep my eye on that door.

>   *They move to a back table facing the front door.*
>   *FRANK arms himself with an empty quart*
>   *bottle of beer. JACKIE picks up his cuestick*
>   *from the floor. They sit looking at the door.*

JERRY:
>   Shit, *Montréal Matin*, here we are.

JACKIE: *putting his arms around JERRY and FRANK*
>   Hey, it's good to know the guys from the Point can
>   still stick together.

FRANK:
>   Yeah, like glue. Crazy Glue.

JACKIE:
>   Oh, yeah, Frank, before I forget, we're gonna have a
>   party on Saturday night.

FRANK:
>   Ha ha. Goody gumdrops.

>   *JERRY drinks down the last glass of beer on*
>   *the table.*

JERRY:
>   Well, that's it, eh? What do ya say, we split over to
>   my place, eh?

JACKIE:
>   Two more rounds.

JERRY:
>   Shit.

JACKIE: *yelling*
Claude. Hey, Claude. Where the fuck is he?

*CLAUDE comes around the corner with
CHABOUGAMOU tagging behind him carrying
his shopping bag full of empty bottles.*

Hey, Claude, put six more beers on the table.
Emergency rations.

CLAUDE:
No beer for you.

JACKIE:
What?

CLAUDE:
No beer. You drink that and you go.

JACKIE:
What's that?

CLAUDE:
No fighting in here.

JACKIE:
I didn't start the fuckin' fight.

CLAUDE:
That's not my fault.

JACKIE:
Hey, what is this?

CLAUDE:
That's the law.

CHABOUGAMOU: *echoing him*
That's the law.

JACKIE:
>
> Chabougamou can drink and I can't?

CLAUDE:
>
> That's not the same thing.

CHABOUGAMOU:
>
> Not the same thing.

CLAUDE:
>
> Chabougamou, he don't fight.

FRANK:
>
> Yeah, but he pisses himself.

CLAUDE:
>
> When he do that, I throw him out.

CHABOUGAMOU:
>
> I throw him out.

JACKIE:
>
> Hey, fuck, what is this?

CLAUDE:
>
> It's true, I throw him out.

CHABOUGAMOU:
>
> It's true.

JACKIE:
>
> Look, fuck Chabougamou! Gimme some beer.

CLAUDE:
>
> No beer. Sorry, no beer.

> *He walks away from the table.*

CHABOUGAMOU:
>
> Hey, Claude, attend peu.

JACKIE:
I don't believe it.

CHABOUGAMOU:
Hey, Claude.

He opens his shopping bag and starts putting the empty soft drink bottles on the table.

Trois bières, Claude.

CLAUDE:
C'est pas l'argent, tabarnac!

CHABOUGAMOU:
Oui, Claude. Oui, les bouteilles. C'est l'argent. C'est l'argent.

CLAUDE:
Okay, okay, une bière.

CHABOUGAMOU:
Deux, Claude. Deux bières.

CLAUDE: *putting down one beer on CHABOUGAMOU's table and picking up the empty bottles* Une bière. Now don't bother me no more.

JACKIE:
I don't fuckin' believe it, man. I'm gonna leave this province, I swear.

CHABOUGAMOU: *sitting down with his beer*
Pas la même chose.

JACKIE:
Shut up or I'll fuckin' hammer ya.

CHABOUGAMOU:
Not the same thing.

FRANK:

    Hey, I think I'll go over there and, uh, tell the guys about the Bouchers.

JACKIE:

    You're coming back, eh, Frank?

FRANK:

    Yeah, yeah.

    GROS GAS enters and JACKIE, JERRY and FRANK jump.

GROS GAS:

    Hey, Jacques. Hey, Jacques, mon vieux.

JACKIE:

    Aw, shit.

GROS GAS:

    Hey, bon homme, you did it, eh? Sacrement!

    He hugs him.

JACKIE:

    Ouch, the head. Hey, watch the head, tabarnac!

GROS GAS:

    Hey, câlice, you beat me to it. The best thing that happen this year. Hey, Frank, he did it, eh?

FRANK:

    Yeah, he sure did.

    GROS GAS takes a chair and sits down.

GROS GAS:

    Hey, all the guys want to see you. That's your truck blocking up the dock, eh?

JACKIE:
>Yeah.

GROS GAS:
>Good.

JACKIE:
>Good?

GROS GAS:
>Keep it there.

JACKIE:
>Hey, fuck, somebody finally agrees with me.

GROS GAS:
>Sure, keep it there. All this trouble is bringing the guys together.

JACKIE:
>Ya gonna stick around a while, Gas?

GROS GAS:
>I think we're gonna walk out.

FRANK:
>A walkout?

GROS GAS:
>Something like that. Even old Fred is thinking about it. All they need is a push. So, Jackie, bon homme, come on with me and push.

JACKIE:
>Forget it.

GROS GAS:
>After your beer?

JACKIE:
>Forget it. I ain't walking out.

98

GROS GAS:

>Hey, Jacques.

JACKIE:

>Look, man, I'm tired of walking in and out, in and out like a fuckin' revolving door. You walk out. I'm staying here.

GROS GAS:

>Jacques.

JACKIE:

>I don't need the grief.

FRANK:

>Hey, did ya talk to Murray?

GROS GAS:

>Murray? He don't think it's the right time, but if the guys want to walk out now, it must be the right time, eh? Hey, Jacques, let's go.

FRANK:

>Yeah, let's go, Jackie.

JERRY:

>They need ya over there, man.

JACKIE:

>My head is sore. Don't bother me right now.

GROS GAS:

>You and me, Jacques, we did it before.

JACKIE:

>Yeah, I know, and what happened, eh? What happened, Gas?

GROS GAS:

>We lost.

JACKIE:
    Yeah, we lost.

GROS GAS:
    So, one more time, Jacques. Maybe this time.

JACKIE:
    Hey, I'm sick of pushing those guys, man. Let them
    do it themselves.

GROS GAS:
    The squareheads won't listen to me. I need you,
    Jacques.

JACKIE:
    Gas, I'm trying to tell ya, it's your turn, man.

GROS GAS:
    What's wrong, Jacques?

JACKIE:
    Nothing's wrong with me, man. I'm alright.

GROS GAS: *sighing*
    You won't move that truck?

JACKIE:
    Don't worry.

GROS GAS:
    For sure?

JACKIE:
    For sure.

GROS GAS:
    Bon. Okay, see you later. Salut.

        He heads towards the door.

FRANK:
> Hey, Gas, the foreman's got friends. Keep your eyes
> open, eh?

GROS GAS:
> Oui.

JACKIE:
> Hey, Gas. Attend peu.

GROS GAS:
> Oui?

JACKIE:
> Do me a favour, will ya? Sit over there and order six
> bières?

GROS GAS:
> Sit over there? Pourquoi?

JACKIE:
> 'Cause Claude . . . Look, just do it for me, okay?

> *He hands him some money.*

GROS GAS:
> Over there! Six bières?

JACKIE:
> Yeah, thanks.

GROS GAS:
> Claude. Hey, Claude.

FRANK:
> This is crazy.

JACKIE:
> What's crazy?

FRANK:
 This whole fuckin' thing.

JACKIE:
 You don't like it, the door's over there.

FRANK:
 Yeah, eh?

JACKIE:
 Yeah.

JERRY:
 I think ya oughta go over there with Gros Gas, man.
 I mean, uh, I agree, walkouts are not the answer,
 but . . .

JACKIE:
 Forget it.

JERRY:
 We can't just sit here.

GROS GAS:
 Hey, Claude.

JERRY:
 Jackie, this don't make any sense.

 CLAUDE enters with some beer on his tray.

CLAUDE:
 Quoi?

GROS GAS:
 Six bières.

CLAUDE:
 Six? Six?

GROS GAS:
> Oui, six. J'ai soif.

> *CLAUDE puts six beers on his table and GROS GAS pays him.*

CLAUDE:
> Six beers. You don't work today? Merci.

> *He passes by JACKIE's table.*

> You like it here?

> *He exits.*

JACKIE:
> Hey, Gas, bring that beer over here.

> *GROS GAS picks up the table and brings it over.*

GROS GAS:
> Here we go again.

> *He sits down with them.*

FRANK:
> Wonder what's keeping the Bouchers, eh? Maybe they can't find the place.

JACKIE:
> They're probably just busy, Frank.

FRANK:
> Yeah, fuck, gotta kill somebody else first.

> *The telephone rings. FRANK goes over and answers it.*

> Yeah, hullo? No, Murray still ain't here. Me? I'm Frank. Frank Saladini. Yeah, that's right, you don't know me. Who are you? Yeah? I don't know you

either. Hey, is it true our union dues are going up this June? Hey, hullo? Hullo?

He hangs up the telephone.

That's Murray's boss again, all choked up over something.

JACKIE: *sniffing*
Hey, check Chabougamou. He's got the shakes.

FRANK:
Hey, Chabougamou, you okay?

JERRY:
Jackie.

JACKIE:
Here, pass him this beer, Frank.

FRANK goes over to CHABOUGAMOU.

FRANK:
Hey, Chabougamou. Hey, Rivière du Loup. Here, medicine. Medicine.

CHABOUGAMOU takes a gulp of the beer.

Good, eh? Good. Ça marche bien, eh? You'll be okay. He'll be okay.

JACKIE: *sniffing again*
Hey, Frank, I think he pissed himself.

FRANK: *looking under the table*
I think you're right.

CHABOUGAMOU starts to cry.

CHABOUGAMOU:
No, no. I don't want to. Je ne veux pas. No.

JACKIE:
> Aw, fuck, he's reached the crying stage. Fuck, I hate that, when they cry. Hey, shut up!

CHABOUGAMOU:
> I go now. I go.

FRANK:
> Yeah, you'll go alright, soon as Claude gets a whiff of you.

> *MURRAY enters. JACKIE, JERRY and FRANK jump. FRANK slips and falls on the floor. He is holding an empty quart bottle of beer.*

JACKIE:
> Murray.

MURRAY: *looking behind him*
> Hey, what's happening?

FRANK:
> Murray.

MURRAY:
> Noisy out there, huh? You lose something, Frank?

FRANK: *getting up off the floor*
> No. I thought you were someone else, okay?

MURRAY:
> So, Jack, I heard you resolved the foreman question all by yourself. Humm, lemme look at this.

> *He studies JACKIE's bruised face.*

> Humm, it's an improvement.

JACKIE:
> Yeah, he looks better too.

MURRAY:
>Yeah, I can imagine.

GROS GAS:
>So, Murray, did you talk to the bosses?

>>*MURRAY sits down and opens his health food lunch.*

MURRAY:
>Where do you think I've been all afternoon?

GROS GAS:
>Yeah, so?

MURRAY:
>So, they gave me the "why didn't ya tell us routine" and then, after offering myself as human sacrifice, they decided that "yes, maybe it was possible to have the foreman transferred."

GROS GAS:
>Transferred?

JACKIE:
>I already transferred him.

MURRAY:
>So, everything was settled, but now, how am I gonna explain this?

FRANK:
>They oughta fire the guy.

JACKIE:
>Yeah, that guy's psycho, man.

MURRAY:
>Right, but that's the best I can do for now, eh? I mean, George Roman, the general manager, what can I say?

FRANK:
Yeah, he's a real shit.

MURRAY:
A double shit.

GROS GAS:
Did you tell them to get off our backs?

MURRAY:
Yeah, I told them, Gas.

GROS GAS:
So?

MURRAY:
So, one thing at a time, eh, Gas? I'm not Superman.

GROS GAS:
Yeah, one thing at a time.

MURRAY:
But stalling your truck, Jack, that's another story.
They can get your ass for that.

JACKIE:
Fuck them!

MURRAY:
Yeah, okay.

JACKIE:
Fuck you too, man!

MURRAY:
Right, so you're having one of your moods, huh, but
they'll still get your ass if ya don't move that truck.

GROS GAS:
That truck stays there, eh, Jacques?

JACKIE:
Look, the name's not Jacques, Jack or Jacky with a
"y." It's J-a-c-k-i-e, Jackie.

MURRAY:
Right.

FRANK:
Let's drink up, eh?

GROS GAS:
Oui, let's go. Fred wants to see you, Murray.

MURRAY:
What for?

GROS GAS:
The guys still wanna meeting.

MURRAY:
Okay, what are they doing right now?

GROS GAS:
Sitting around.

MURRAY:
Sitting, huh?

GROS GAS:
Yeah, the dock is blocked off. No work to do.

MURRAY: *sighing*
Yeah, alright, Gas. Tell Fred I'll be over there soon as
I finish eating.

GROS GAS: *exiting*
Okay. Hey, Jacques, Jackie with the "i-e," don't
move that truck.

FRANK:
Hey, Gas. Keep your eyes open, eh?

GROS GAS:
 Eh? Yeah, okay. Salut.

 He exits.

MURRAY:
 Jack, Jackie, you gotta move that truck.

JACKIE:
 What truck?

MURRAY:
 Look, I understand how ya feel, but . . . Hey, what if
 I have the truck towed away, eh? I'll tell Roman it
 broke down. How's that, eh?

JACKIE:
 You talk to Gas about that.

MURRAY:
 Right, okay, Jackie, I'll talk to Gas, don't worry.

JACKIE:
 I'm not worried.

MURRAY:
 Good.

FRANK:
 Wanna beer? Take a beer.

MURRAY:
 No.

JACKIE:
 Here, come on, fuck the diet.

 He puts a beer in front of MURRAY.

MURRAY:

>No, man, that stuff's full of chemicals. That's not a glass, that's a test tube.

FRANK:

>Cottage cheese, yogurt, yuk. How can ya stand that stuff?

MURRAY:

>I don't eat it for the taste, Frank.

JACKIE:

>That's for sure.

FRANK:

>Murray here is a health nut.

JERRY:

>Crunchy granola, eh?

JACKIE:

>Yeah. Hey, Murray, this is Jerry Nines, the guy I told ya about.

JERRY:

>Say, Murray.

MURRAY:

>Oh, yeah, the writer. I've seen your play.

JERRY:

>Yeah?

MURRAY:

>Seen you on TV too.

FRANK:

>Fuckin' funny or what, eh?

JERRY:

>Yeah, well, star of the silver screen. That's me.

MURRAY:
>Marxist with a capital "M," eh?

JERRY:
>Yeah, well, Marxist-Deleonist.

MURRAY:
>Deleonist. That's a rare variety.

FRANK:
>Murray's a commie too.

MURRAY:
>Machiavellian Marxist.

JERRY:
>Machiavellian, yeah.

JACKIE:
>Hey, what did ya think of the play, Murray?

MURRAY:
>The what?

JACKIE:
>The play.

MURRAY:
>Oh, the play, uh, the rhythm was good.

JACKIE: *singing*
>I got rhythm, I got rhythm . . .

JERRY:
>Got an "A" in English, eh?

MURRAY:
>Hey, don't get me wrong. I liked it.

>*JERRY exits to the washroom.*

MURRAY:
>
> What's with him?

JACKIE:
>
> He's got piles.

MURRAY:
>
> Humm, that's a bad eye you got there, Jack. Ya oughta have it checked for concussion. I'm serious.

JACKIE:
>
> Yeah.

MURRAY:
>
> Yeah. Hey, kid, it's been months, huh? Keep meaning to drop by with some hash, man. Miss those stoned evenings.

JACKIE:
>
> Union keeps ya busy, eh?

MURRAY:
>
> Yeah, spring contract.

FRANK:
>
> Up there with the big shots now, eh, Murray? Gonna get yourself a big stomach and a big cigar.

MURRAY:
>
> Not me, Frank, not on cottage cheese.

JACKIE:
>
> I don't know how you put up with those goofs in the union, man.

MURRAY:
>
> I don't.

JACKIE:
>
> Good, it might be contagious.

MURRAY:

> Believe it or not, there's some good guys in the union.

JACKIE:

> I don't believe it.

MURRAY:

> You want to meet them?

> *JERRY re-enters.*

JACKIE:

> Come on, man, I've been to those union meetings and
> it's always the same old fuckers up there telling us
> the union needs this and the company needs that and
> for us to be patient and understanding, and then they
> move this and second that, and any questions? And,
> yeah, I put up my hand, "Yeah, hey, how come we
> always gotta be so fuckin' understanding, eh?" I
> don't pay union dues to be fuckin' understanding.
> You were there, right?

MURRAY:

> Yeah, you really shook them up.

JACKIE:

> Yeah, well, they never picked me again, man, 'cause
> I asked the wrong questions. They only want to hear
> the same bullshit they give us.

FRANK:

> I second that emotion.

JERRY:

> You guys need a new union, man.

JACKIE:

> Yeah, the movie never changes.

MURRAY:

Well, that's no longer true. For example, the Lapalme drivers strike. Well, there we succeeded in pressuring the bureaucrats beyond their usual procedures and . . .

JERRY:

You'll never get nowhere working from the inside, man.

MURRAY:

Uh, well, in that strike, we, uh . . .

FRANK:

What's that you're eating?

MURRAY:

We, uh, pushed for meaningful negotiations and . . .

FRANK:

Raisin bread?

MURRAY:

Whole wheat germ bread. Real bread. Have a piece, Frank. The Lapalme drivers strike was . . .

FRANK:

Hey, I quit using coffee creamers after Murray here told me what was in them. Sodium cas . . . casi . . .

MURRAY:

Sodium caseinate, potassium phosphate, diabasic, monoglycerides, diglycerides, sodium aluminum silicate, plus artificial flavours and colours.

JACKIE:

Yummy, yummy.

FRANK:

Finger licking good.

MURRAY:
> You'd probably shit yourself if I told ya what was in
> those junk cakes you're always eating, Frank.

FRANK:
> What's in them?

MURRAY:
> White sugar.

FRANK:
> White sugar?

MURRAY:
> One of the major causes of cancer and schizophrenia.

FRANK:
> White sugar?

JERRY: *groaning*
> Oh, no.

JACKIE:
> You're kidding?

MURRAY:
> Nope.

FRANK:
> Shitso . . . what?

MURRAY:
> Schizophrenia.

JERRY:
> Hey, I heard brown rice causes paranoia.

MURRAY:
> What?

JERRY:
This whole system causes schizophrenia, man.

MURRAY:
Okay, so be cynical, but thirty years from now, I'll still be getting my nooky while you guys putz around, ass around your ankles.

The telephone starts ringing.

JACKIE:
That's for you, Murray.

MURRAY:
Huh? The office, huh?

He goes over to answer the telephone.

FRANK:
Hey, imagine putzing around with your ass on your ankles.

MURRAY: *on the telephone*
Yes, John, yes. You finally got me. What? What Mini-Loto? Mini-Loto?

JACKIE, JERRY and FRANK laugh.

Must have been the wrong number, John. Must have been. Yeah, yeah, I know there's a truck blocking up the dock. They phoned, huh? Ahuh. Yes, John, I realize a confrontation right now would really screw us up. Ahuh . . .

JACKIE: *to JERRY*
Murray got a little heavy with ya, eh?

JERRY:
Aw, he's a goof, man.

JACKIE:
> Murray's alright, man. He's solid.

FRANK:
> Yeah, he's alright . . . most of the time.

JERRY:
> Yeah, munching on granola while the world falls apart.

JACKIE:
> He stood by us before. I mean, sometimes he gets spaced out with his busy, busy trip, but he's, uh, solid.

FRANK:
> Yeah, Murray's alright. Sometimes he's too smart, but, uh . . .

JACKIE:
> I've talked to him and . . .

FRANK:
> Outfox the fox, ya know? Too smart, but, uh . . .

JACKIE:
> Hey, Frank, dummy up!

FRANK:
> What's with you?

JACKIE:
> I'm talking.

FRANK:
> Yeah, so go ahead, talk. Talk. Me, I'm drinking my beer and I'm going, man.

JACKIE:
> Yeah? Goodbye, Frank.

CHABOUGAMOU:
>C'est pas vrai. Pas vrai. Me, I know. I know.

FRANK:
>Hey, shut your face, okay?

CLAUDE: *entering*
>Hey, hey, the table.

JACKIE:
>Hey, we're redecorating.

CLAUDE:
>Put it back, put it back.

JACKIE:
>Yeah, yeah.

>*JERRY and FRANK move the table back.*

MURRAY: *still on the telephone*
>No problem, alright? It's solved, John. There won't
>be no walkout, okay? Okay, John? Don't worry. You
>want the dock number over there. It's, uh, 931 . . . 28.
>Uh, Jackie, is that 2831 or 2834 over there?

JACKIE:
>I dunno, man.

FRANK:
>2834.

MURRAY:
>It's 2834.

FRANK: *grinning*
>I dunno either.

MURRAY:
>Got that? Right.

>*He hangs up the telephone.*

>Shit, how serious is Gros Gas about walking out?

JACKIE:
>Who knows?

MURRAY:
>What's happening over there?

FRANK:
>It's like a walkout that won't walk out.

MURRAY:
>Jackie, we've got to stop this.

JACKIE:
>Stop what?

MURRAY:
>They're gonna break our contract.

JACKIE:
>So what? They deserve a holiday.

FRANK:
>They deserve a medal.

MURRAY:
>Jackie.

JACKIE:
>If they wanna go play on the merry-go-round, let them.

MURRAY:
>Jackie, what's this? What are you doing?

FRANK:
> Why you so worried, Murray? They walked out
> before.

MURRAY:
> Why am I so worried? Listen, number one, it's illegal.
> That means they're gonna fine the shit out of the
> union. Number two, this disruption is gonna fuck up
> any chances of a good spring contract, and number
> three, and listen carefully . . . Number three, the
> company don't give a damn if you walk out now,
> because they're overstocked, understand? Over-
> stocked. That means they'd love you to walk out
> now. They'll blow kisses.

FRANK:
> Did ya tell Gros Gas that?

MURRAY:
> Sure, but the schmuck's not listening to me. You're
> the hero of the day, Jackie. They'll listen to you.

JACKIE:
> Better find another hero, man.

MURRAY:
> Look, all you got to do is go over there with me and
> tell them to relax.

JACKIE:
> Forget it.

MURRAY:
> Hey, what is this forget it crap, huh? Did we bust our
> ass to get a union or what? You remember how much
> trouble that was?

JACKIE:
> You're not listening, man.

MURRAY:

Look, one more hassle from this local and they're gonna kick us out, and that means no union, no protection, no nothing. Back down on our knees begging.

JACKIE:

I've had it, man. I don't need the grief.

MURRAY:

Look, give the union a chance. Push them, bug them, make it work.

JACKIE:

How, Murray?

MURRAY:

Look, by being at the meetings, by voting . . .

JACKIE:

Be patient and understanding, eh?

MURRAY:

I'm trying to tell ya . . .

JACKIE:

Forget it. I got it.

MURRAY:

What other choice have we got? I mean, this is it, our only means of defence an you wanna throw it away.

JACKIE:

Fuck the defence! I wanna attack, man.

JERRY:

That's right, man.

MURRAY: *sighing*
Fuck! Okay, what's happening? You're not happy, right? You don't like the job and ya don't like the union. You're not happy, right?

JACKIE:
Don't play games, Murray.

MURRAY:
Who's playing games? What is this? Kamikaze or what? . . . Frank, gimme one of those beers.

He takes a slug of beer.

Well, that's it. Now it's gonna take me another three months to get back on my diet. You guys drive me crazy, ya know that?

FRANK:
Welcome to the club.

MURRAY:
It's not easy being a health nut around you guys. Gimme a smoke, Frank.

FRANK:
You sure?

MURRAY:
Come on, come on. Gimme a smoke.

FRANK throws him a cigarette. He lights it.

Five months, five months, I kept my body pure and beautiful. Now look at me. I hope ya feel bad.

JACKIE:
Aw, shut up.

MURRAY:
Ya klutz. So what are we gonna do now? Just sit here and watch the shit hit the fan or what?

To JERRY.

Hey, Marxist, you're his friend. Why don't ya talk to him?

JERRY:
I think he's right, man. Fuck the defence. You oughta attack, man.

MURRAY:
But he don't want to walk out.

JACKIE:
Yeah. Forget it, man.

JERRY:
No, don't walk out. Walk back in.

MURRAY:
What?

JERRY:
Just take over the warehouse and tell the bosses to walk out. A sitdown strike.

JACKIE:
I don't get it.

JERRY:
Well, it might not work on a small scale, but, uh, remember back in the Sixties when the students were taking over administration buildings?

JACKIE:
Yeah.

JERRY:

Well, they had the right idea, man. Stay where your
strength is. Why go out in the street where ya got no
power. Let the bosses come to you.

MURRAY:

Not that campus crap.

JACKIE:

We stay, they go, eh?

MURRAY:

It won't work, man.

JERRY:

Why not? This way, you don't hafta worry about
overstock or your fuckin' union contract. You'll be
right there in control, man.

JACKIE:

We stay, they go. I like it, Murray.

JERRY:

Yeah, let them come to you, man.

MURRAY:

Jackie, you try something like that and the cops are
gonna string ya up by the balls.

JACKIE:

Yeah, we just go over there and tell them to get the
fuck out, right? They walk out.

JERRY:

Right. Worker's control of the industries.

MURRAY:

Oh, no. Can I design the flag?

JACKIE:

What do ya think, Frankie?

124

FRANK:
   Me? I wanna go home.

JACKIE:
   Frankie, it's a way out, man.

FRANK:
   Aw, I dunno, man. I dunno.

JACKIE:
   Remember Ti-Jean? Now's our chance.

MURRAY:
   Jackie.

JACKIE:
   I like it, man.

MURRAY:
   Look, get serious. It's all candy shit, man. Candy shit.
   Stick your finger up your ass and put it in your
   mouth, man. Candy shit. He's gonna have fun playing
   Karl Marx while you guys get your heads kicked in . . .
   And for what? That pie in the sky crap?

JERRY:
   Listen, you wanna live like this, you go ahead, man.

MURRAY:
   Somebody talking to you?

JERRY:
   You live off this garbage, eh? It keeps you busy.

   He pushes MURRAY.

MURRAY: *pushing JERRY back*
   Hey, I'm a lover, not a fighter.

   *JERRY and MURRAY start swinging at each
   other. JACKIE and FRANK break it up.*

125

JACKIE:
> Hey, Jerry. Jerry, what's the matter? Your socks are dirty. Ya got dirty socks.

JERRY:
> I'm tired of goofs, man.

JACKIE:
> Cool it, man. It don't look good on you.

MURRAY:
> Hey, what's with that guy? Fuck off, Frank!

> *He pushes FRANK away.*

JACKIE:
> Hey, look, we gotta work this out. Murray, I like the idea.

MURRAY:
> Count me out.

JACKIE:
> Frank, it's gonna work.

FRANK:
> I need a coffee.

JERRY:
> Coffee, yeah. Let's get sobered up, man.

JACKIE:
> Yeah.

> *GROS GAS and FRED enter. JACKIE, JERRY and FRANK jump.*

GROS GAS:
> We got them. We got them. The Bouchers.

FRANK:
Ya got them?

JACKIE:
Yeah?

GROS GAS:
We jumped like that. Not a chance. Fini. Me, I got just this.

He shows them a small bruise on his arm.

JACKIE:
Hey, fuck, too much!

FRANK:
Yeah, have a beer.

GROS GAS:
Thanks. Go on, Fred, tell him.

FRED:
You tell him.

GROS GAS:
Go on, Fred.

FRED:
Alright, Jackie, Gros Gas wants me to tell you that we're walking out even if I don't want to, because nearly everybody else does.

MURRAY:
Fred.

GROS GAS:
Just some of the squareheads don't want to.

FRED:
Yeah, like me, but anyhow, we voted and we're walking out.

GROS GAS:
> They want you over there, Jacques.

MURRAY:
> Fred, I want to talk to you.

GROS GAS:
> Don't listen to him, Fred.

MURRAY:
> Fred.

FRED:
> They're walking out, Murray.

JACKIE:
> Well, I'm not walking out.

GROS GAS:
> Not walking out, but . . .

FRANK:
> We're walking in.

GROS GAS:
> Walking in?

JACKIE:
> Yeah, we stay, they go. We're gonna make the bosses
> walk out.

MURRAY:
> I don't believe it.

GROS GAS:
> We stay, they go? The bosses walk out? Hey, Fred.

FRED:
> Oh, no.

MURRAY:
>Oh, yeah.

JACKIE:
>Yeah, it's called, uh . . .

JERRY:
>Sitdown strike.

JACKIE:
>Yeah, a sitdown strike.

GROS GAS:
>We stay, they go. Hey, I like that, Fred.

FRED:
>What's the union gonna do?

MURRAY:
>Who cares? You don't need a union, you need a
>psychiatrist.

JACKIE:
>Come on, Gas, first thing we gotta do is have a
>meeting and Jerry here will talk to the guys, right?

JERRY:
>Well, I'm not much of a speaker, but, uh . . .

JACKIE:
>You'll do okay. Then, Gas, we're gonna go up to that
>office, man, and . . .

>*MURRAY stops JACKIE's exit.*

MURRAY:
>Jackie.

JACKIE:
>You coming, Murray?

MURRAY:

Jackie, get serious, man. They're gonna slaughter ya.

JACKIE:

We got nothing to lose, man.

MURRAY:

It's crazy, Jackie, it really is.

GROS GAS:

Hey, Jacques, come on.

JACKIE:

You're in my way, man.

CLAUDE enters.

MURRAY:

Look, Jackie, wait. Listen. Listen, you guys. If you're gonna do this, do it right, okay? Do it right and wait till Thursday.

FRANK:

Thursday?

MURRAY:

Yeah, do it Thursday and then you'll get publicity in the weekend papers. They'll make a big deal out of it.

JACKIE:

Let's go.

MURRAY:

Wait, it's better that way. Wait.

He tries to stop JACKIE again.

JACKIE:

Fuck off!

JACKIE pushes him out of the way.

130

Hey, Frank, come on.

JACKIE exits with JERRY, GROS GAS and FRED.

FRANK:
Yeah, yeah.

FRANK picks up a beer from the table.

CLAUDE:
Hey, Frank, put it back.

FRANK:
It's okay. We paid for it.

CLAUDE:
You drink it here. No beer to go.

FRANK: *putting the beer down on the table*
Hey, then Chabougamou's gonna get it.

CLAUDE:
Don't worry about that.

CHABOUGAMOU:
Don't worry about that.

FRANK exits.

CLAUDE: *handing CHABOUGAMOU the beer*
Here, go sit in the back. Là-bas.

CHABOUGAMOU:
Merci. Là-bas, Claude.

CLAUDE:
Oui, là-bas. Further than that.

CHABOUGAMOU: *sitting down*
Okay, Claude?

131

MURRAY: *at the pool table*
I don't believe it. They're going on strike. It's crazy.

CLAUDE:
Aw, strike one, strike two, strike three. They lose all the time, like the Expos.

The telephone rings.

That's for you.

MURRAY:
Huh?

CLAUDE:
That's for you.

MURRAY: *going over and answering the telephone*
Yeah, it's for me alright. Hullo? Hullo, John. Yeah, no, they're not walking out, they're having a sitdown strike. Yeah, they decided that would be more fun. Yeah, what? Make a statement to the papers? No, John, they're crazy, but I can't do that, John. No, no, forget it, John. John? John, are you listening, John? Fuck you, John! That's right, fuck you! What? No, I don't want to discuss it.

He hangs up the telephone.

I am screwed. I lost my job, I'm off my diet . . .

CLAUDE: *looking up from his newspaper*
Tabarnac!

MURRAY:
You're off your diet?

CLAUDE:
Hey, me, look, I'm just four numbers off the Mini-Loto. Maudit Christ!

MURRAY:
My heart bleeds.

CHABOUGAMOU:
Mini-Loto?

He pulls out his wallet.

Mini-Loto, I win? Hey, Claude, I win?

CLAUDE:
You got a ticket?

CHABOUGAMOU:
I win?

CLAUDE: *looking at CHABOUGAMOU's ticket*
Donne moi ça. Hey, Christ, it's two years old.

CHABOUGAMOU:
I win?

CLAUDE:
You lose. Out! Va-t-en! You piss yourself, out!

He bounces CHABOUGAMOU out.
CHABOUGAMOU bumps into FRANK,
who is entering.

FRANK:
Hey, watch it.

CLAUDE:
Not my fault. You came in the wrong door.

FRANK:
Hey, the other door is broken.

CLAUDE: *sitting down with his newspaper*
Not my fault.

FRANK:
>Fuck, hey, Murray, Jackie wants to know when you're coming over.

MURRAY:
>He does, huh?

FRANK:
>Yeah, there's this goof from the *Star* over there and nobody knows how to talk to him.

MURRAY:
>What about hotshot, the writer?

FRANK:
>Him? He told the guy to fuck off.

MURRAY:
>Yeah, right. He would.

FRANK:
>Yeah, but the guy loved it.

MURRAY:
>New approach, huh?

FRANK:
>Yeah, so, uh, Jackie told me to tell you to, uh, quit sulking and get over there 'cause, uh, you're the only guy who knows how to talk to goofs.

MURRAY:
>Who's sulking?

FRANK:
>Well, uh, Jackie didn't tell me to say you were sulking, he, uh . . . You coming over or what?

MURRAY:
>How can I resist?

FRANK:
 Yeah, come on.

MURRAY:
 So, what am I supposed to say?

FRANK:
 You'll think of something.

MURRAY:
 I'll think of something.

FRANK:
 You coming?

MURRAY: *getting up to exit*
 Alright, but I'm not saying I'm gonna stay there.
 I like my nose the way it is.

FRANK:
 Okay, okay. Hey, uh, sorry I said you were sulking,
 uh . . .

MURRAY:
 Do me a favour, Frank. Shut up. First thing we gotta
 do is phone the CBC. We'll call it a social experiment.

FRANK:
 Yeah, yeah. Don't worry, Murray, you'll confuse
 them.

 They exit and CHABOUGAMOU enters.

CLAUDE:
 Hey, hey, out!

CHABOUGAMOU:
 My ticket.

CLAUDE:
 Out!

CHABOUGAMOU:
My ticket.

> *CLAUDE struggles with CHABOUGAMOU at the door of the tavern. The factory whistle blows louder and much longer than usual. They freeze.*

Tabarnac!

CLAUDE:
I never hear the whistle blow like that, you?

CHABOUGAMOU:
Non . . . My ticket.

> *CLAUDE lets CHABOUGAMOU loose and he goes over and picks up his Mini-Loto ticket from the floor.*

CLAUDE:
Okay, Ti-Cul, now you go, eh? You drink too much today, eh? You go, come back tomorrow, eh, bon homme?

> *CHABOUGAMOU exits and the factory whistle blows again, louder and longer than before. CLAUDE shakes his head and begins to clear the tables.*

Must be that Jackie. Crazy guy, crazy guy.

> *He exits the other side of the tavern carrying a tray full of empty glasses.*